Swift iOS Programming for Kids

Unleash your child's developer potential through fun projects and help them learn how to create iOS apps in Swift

Steffen D. Sommer
Jim Campagno

BIRMINGHAM - MUMBAI

Swift iOS Programming for Kids

First published: March 2017

Production reference: 1170317

Published by Packt Publishing Ltd.
Livery Place
35 Livery Street
Birmingham
B32PB, UK.
ISBN 978-1-78712-074-7

www.packtpub.com

Credits

Authors

Steffen D. Sommer

Jim Campagno

Reviewer

Doug Sparling

Commissioning Editor

Ashwin Nair

Acquisition Editor

Shweta Pant

Content Development Editor

Aditi Gour

Technical Editor

Sushant S Nadkar

Copy Editor

Shaila Kusanale

Project Coordinator

Ritika Manoj

Proofreader

Safis Editing

Indexer

Tejal Daruwale Soni

Graphics

Jason Monteiro

Production Coordinator

Melwyn Dsa

About the Authors

Since Swift was announced at WWDC, **Steffen D. Sommer** has had a passionate interest in the programming language. He's currently working as a lead Vapor developer at a company called Nodes in Copenhagen, where he focuses on developing backend systems using Swift.

In his spare time, he helps organize the local iOS meet up, visits iOS conferences around the world, and explores the different aspects of and use cases for Swift, such as putting Swift on the server and doing functional programming in Swift. You can also find him contributing to open source projects on GitHub or blogging on his personal website.

> *First, I would like to thank my girlfriend, Mia, for her never-ending feedback and support while I wrote this book. I would also like to thank my friends at IAIF for their input and support throughout the process.*

Jim Campagno is an iOS developer and teacher living in New York City. He's currently working as an iOS instructor at the Flatiron School, helping beginners of Swift and iOS become iOS developers.

Jim has a deep desire and high level of creativity that he brings to teaching. He created the Swift online course offered at Flatiron School, which includes in-depth readings along with test-driven labs, challenging the student to write code in Swift. Jim also runs an active YouTube channel, putting out in-depth content and helping students understand everything in iOS and Swift—from the basics to complex topics.

Most importantly, Jim ensures that the content he creates is accessible, fun, and interactive. He enjoys putting together a story behind every topic to make it more enjoyable for the reader.

> *I would like to thank my roommates (Tom and Matt) for putting up with me while I wrote this book. I would also like to thank Tim Clem, who has inspired me to keep learning. Lastly, I would like to thank Joe Burgess for teaching me how to code.*

About the Reviewer

Doug Sparling works as a technical architect and software developer for Andrews McMeel Universal, a publishing and syndication company in Kansas City, MO. At AMU, he uses Go for web services, Python for backend services, Ruby on Rails and WordPress for website development, and Objective-C, Swift, and Java for native iOS and Android development. AMU's sites include `www.gocomics.com`, `www.uexpress.com`, `www.puzzlesociety.com`, and `dilbert.com`.

He also was the co-author of a Perl book, *Instant Perl Modules* for *McGraw-Hill*, and a reviewer for other Packt Publishing books, including *jQuery 2.0 Animation Techniques: Beginner's Guide* and *WordPress Web Application Development*. Doug has also played various roles for Manning Publications as reviewer, technical development editor, and proofer, working on books such as *Go in Action*, *The Well-Grounded Rubyist 2nd Edition*, *iOS Development with Swift*, and *Programming for Musicians and Digital Artists*.

www.PacktPub.com

For support files and downloads related to your book, please visit www.PacktPub.com.

Did you know that Packt offers eBook versions of every book published, with PDF and ePub files available? You can upgrade to the eBook version at www.PacktPub.com and as a print book customer, you are entitled to a discount on the eBook copy. Get in touch with us at service@packtpub.com for more details.

At www.PacktPub.com, you can also read a collection of free technical articles, sign up for a range of free newsletters and receive exclusive discounts and offers on Packt books and eBooks.

https://www.packtpub.com/mapt

Get the most in-demand software skills with Mapt. Mapt gives you full access to all Packt books and video courses, as well as industry-leading tools to help you plan your personal development and advance your career.

Why subscribe?

- Fully searchable across every book published by Packt
- Copy and paste, print, and bookmark content
- On demand and accessible via a web browser

Customer Feedback

Thanks for purchasing this Packt book. At Packt, quality is at the heart of our editorial process. To help us improve, please leave us an honest review on this book's Amazon page at https://www.amazon.com/Swift-Programming-Kids-Steffen-Sommer/dp/1787120740/.

If you'd like to join our team of regular reviewers, you can e-mail us at customerreviews@packtpub.com. We award our regular reviewers with free eBooks and videos in exchange for their valuable feedback. Help us be relentless in improving our products!

Table of Contents

Preface

Swift has risen quickly to be one of the preferred languages among developers and will have a long and fruitful future under the guidance of Apple. Since making the language open source over a year ago, it's become clear that Swift will be a versatile cross-platform language with a wealth of opportunities beyond Apple's ecosystem.

This book will introduce you to programming in a fun and approachable way. We will be building and interacting with fun examples to help you grasp multiple concepts. We will also be building fun iOS applications to help solidify your knowledge of Swift.

What this book covers

Chapter 1, *What is Programming?*, introduces the Swift programming language.

Chapter 2, *Getting Set up*, shows you how to install Xcode and introduces you to writing code in a Playground file.

Chapter 3, *Say Hello*, helps you create your own Playground file and write your first line of code.

Chapter 4, *Favorite Things*, discusses how to store values in variables and constants.

Chapter 5, *Factories*, explains types and introduces the String and int types.

Chapter 6, *Making Pizza*, outlines the problem that functions solve along with creating your own functions.

Chapter 7, *Toy Bin*, covers the array and dictionary types.

Chapter 8, *Smarter Toy Bin*, focuses on the use of loops and if-else statements.

Chapter 9, *Make Some Friends*, takes you through object-oriented programming and classes. You will create your first instance of a class.

Chapter 10, *Pokémon Battle*, helps you create your own Pokémon class along with having instances of this class interact with each other.

Chapter 11, *Simon Says*, introduces Interface Builder and Storyboards, and also helps you create your first application with a user interface.

Chapter 12, *Starry Night*, showcases the view hierarchy and auto layout. You will be creating an application that has a user interface that scales across multiple screen sizes and that will be able to change its background color at the press of a button.

Chapter 13, *Space Pizza Delivery*, shows you how to create an iOS application that incorporates everything we've learned so far. It also introduces enums, private variables, protocols, delegates, and property observers.

Chapter 14, *Movie Night - iOS App*, takes you through creating an iOS application that introduces UITableViews and persisting data between the launches of the application.

What you need for this book

You will need the following things for the book:

- A Mac computer running OS X 10.11.5 or later.
- The Xcode application, which is available in the Mac App Store for free.
- An iPhone running iOS 8 or newer if you want to test your application on a device. This is optional.

Who this book is for

Children who are curious about the technology we use in our daily lives and who want to know how it works can use this book to learn about programming and build their first iOS app. No prior programming experience is necessary.

Conventions

In this book, you will find a number of text styles that distinguish between different kinds of information. Here are some examples of these styles and an explanation of their meaning.

Code words in text, database table names, folder names, filenames, file extensions, pathnames, dummy URLs, user input, and Twitter handles are shown as follows: "The compiler will expect your variables to be of a certain type (int, string, and so on) and will throw a compile-time error if you try to assign a value of a different type."

A block of code is set as follows:

```
class Pokemon {
    let name: String
    init(name: String) {
```

```
        self.name = name
    }
}
```

New terms and **important words** are shown in bold. Words that you see on the screen, for example, in menus or dialog boxes, appear in the text like this: "Launch Xcode and navigate to **File** | **New** | **Project**."

Warnings or important notes appear in a box like this.

Tips and tricks appear like this.

Reader feedback

Feedback from our readers is always welcome. Let us know what you think about this book-what you liked or disliked. Reader feedback is important for us as it helps us develop titles that you will really get the most out of. To send us general feedback, simply e-mail feedback@packtpub.com, and mention the book's title in the subject of your message. If there is a topic that you have expertise in and you are interested in either writing or contributing to a book, see our author guide at www.packtpub.com/authors.

Customer support

Now that you are the proud owner of a Packt book, we have a number of things to help you to get the most from your purchase.

Downloading the example code

You can download the example code files for this book from your account at http://www.packtpub.com. If you purchased this book elsewhere, you can visit http://www.packtpub.com/support and register to have the files e-mailed directly to you.

You can download the code files by following these steps:

1. Log in or register to our website using your e-mail address and password.
2. Hover the mouse pointer on the **SUPPORT** tab at the top.
3. Click on **Code Downloads & Errata**.
4. Enter the name of the book in the **Search** box.
5. Select the book for which you're looking to download the code files.
6. Choose from the drop-down menu where you purchased this book from.
7. Click on **Code Download**.

Once the file is downloaded, please make sure that you unzip or extract the folder using the latest version of:

- WinRAR / 7-Zip for Windows
- Zipeg / iZip / UnRarX for Mac
- 7-Zip / PeaZip for Linux

The code bundle for the book is also hosted on GitHub at `https://github.com/PacktPublishing/Swift-iOS-Programming-for-Kids`. We also have other code bundles from our rich catalog of books and videos available at `https://github.com/PacktPublishing/`. Check them out!

Downloading the color images of this book

We also provide you with a PDF file that has color images of the screenshots/diagrams used in this book. The color images will help you better understand the changes in the output. You can download this file from `https://www.packtpub.com/sites/default/files/downloads/SwiftiOSProgrammingforKids_ColorImages.pdf`.

Errata

Although we have taken every care to ensure the accuracy of our content, mistakes do happen. If you find a mistake in one of our books-maybe a mistake in the text or the code-we would be grateful if you could report this to us. By doing so, you can save other readers from frustration and help us improve subsequent versions of this book. If you find any errata, please report them by visiting `http://www.packtpub.com/submit-errata`, selecting your book, clicking on the **Errata Submission Form** link, and entering the details of your errata. Once your errata are verified, your submission will be accepted and the errata will be uploaded to our website or added to any list of existing errata under the Errata section of that title.

To view the previously submitted errata, go to `https://www.packtpub.com/books/content/support`and enter the name of the book in the search field. The required information will appear under the **Errata** section.

Piracy

Piracy of copyrighted material on the Internet is an ongoing problem across all media. At Packt, we take the protection of our copyright and licenses very seriously. If you come across any illegal copies of our works in any form on the Internet, please provide us with the location address or website name immediately so that we can pursue a remedy.

Please contact us at `copyright@packtpub.com` with a link to the suspected pirated material.

We appreciate your help in protecting our authors and our ability to bring you valuable content.

Questions

If you have a problem with any aspect of this book, you can contact us at `questions@packtpub.com`, and we will do our best to address the problem.

1
What is Programming?

We use programming to instruct a computer. Computers include smartphones (such as the iPhone), tablets, game consoles (such as the PlayStation), and a lot more. We say that a computer runs a program, which means that when you open your favorite game or application (also referred to as an **app**) on your PlayStation or on your iPhone, the device will know how to interpret and execute the program, which in this case is your game or application. A program is simply a set of *instructions* that your device is able to understand. We can also consider these instructions as a recipe for the device. The recipe will tell your iPhone what your favorite game is all about–everything from the colors of your avatar, to the text in the menus, to what happens when you tap on an enemy or on an animal in a game. This recipe can be written in many ways depending on your personal preference and the device that is supposed to run it. The programming language refers to the language you choose to write your program in.

This chapter will go through the following topics:

- Introducing the Swift programming language
- Why is programming important?
- What the reader can expect from this book

The Swift programming language

Swift is a programming language introduced by Apple, which you can use to create apps for the most common Apple devices, including the iPhone. The language and device you choose defines the possibilities for your program, for example, using Swift and targeting an iPhone as your device, you will be able to access the camera of the iPhone to take photos in your application, or the speaker of the iPhone in order to play sounds in your application. If you choose JavaScript as your programming language, HTML as your markup language and target the browser on your computer as your device, then you will be able to create interactive web pages. A programming language can differ much from language to language, and although the languages can share common concepts, it does not mean that one will master every programming language just by learning one. This leads to what **programming** is: it is the act of creating a program or recipe for your device to run. What is the result? The result is your program, your application, or your game.

Let's imagine this simple application for an iPhone–Movie Night, which has a list of your favorite movies. If the list is longer than the height of your device, you are able to scroll through the list by swiping up and down. You can add movies to your list by tapping a button and entering a name for the movie and you can delete them again by swiping left on the movie in the list. The idea of the app is to keep a list of your favorite movies so that you can remember them when having a movie night. In this case, the program is the application (called Movie Night), the device is the iPhone, and the instructions of the application could be the colors of the background and texts, the list in which you can scroll, and the add and delete functionalities. Programming is about creating these set of instructions so that we are able run our application on our iPhone. If you're excited about creating your own Movie Night app that you can use with your friends, then read along as this is an application we will build together in `Chapter 14`, *Movie Night – iOS App*.

Why is programming important?

There are many reasons for why programming is becoming increasingly popular. The result of doing programming allows people to connect through social media, such as Facebook and Instagram; it allows people to be entertained through immersive and rich games; and it allows people to learn and become educated in a fun and engaging manner using interactive applications. Programming has enabled us to share knowledge across geographical boundaries in a way that seemed impossible before programming existed. Programming has helped us automate tasks such as selling tickets at the local train station, paying in a faster and secure way using our smartphone, and programming has helped us measure the well-being of humans in order to give the right treatment at the right moment.

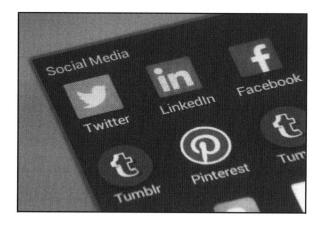

Programming has made it possible for us to instruct a computer on how to perform certain tasks in a more efficient and reliable manner than would ever be possible for a human being. There are natural limits to how much a person can do within the 24 hours of a day or within the lifetime of a person's life. Also, it is costly to have a person perform tedious tasks that seem repetitive, time-consuming, or based on deterministic behavior, such as calculations. As it is costly and it can be hard to find the right or, simply, enough people, it also means that it does not scale very well. Computers are relatively cheap and can be considered as fairly stable. If computers break, they are easy to replace, which means that performing tasks using computers scales really well. Just imagine a bank system without computers; imagine people sitting and keeping track of each person's balance and trying to keep it synchronized across large geographical distances.

Imagine the recent PokÃ©mon smartphone game being done without computers. With no computers, there would need to be maps distributed to each player that show exactly where a PokÃ©mon is located and people (from the game) would need to be at the actual geographical location in order to tell or validate that the PokÃ©mon trainer had just found a PokÃ©mon. Also, in order to keep track of PokÃ©mon caught, and not to mention the outcome of a battle with another trainer, a lot needs to be handled on paper by the player. Without computers, one can easily think of problems with consistent play experiences, such as verifying that a player does not cheat and modifying the game rules as the game evolves, just to name a few. In general, computers have the ability to enhance our daily life, and we quickly forget what the world would look like without computers. Traditionally, programming has had a steep learning curve and, in general, been inaccessible by younger people. Today, programming is widely used and we have many different languages and tools that solve a lot of different types of problems. This means that it has been possible to lower the learning curve and involve people of different ages and with different capabilities.

What you will learn from this book

This book gives you an introduction to the programming language, Swift. Swift is a fairly new programming language (version 1 came out in September 2014) and the language can be used to write programs for most of the Apple devices, including the iPhone, iPad, Apple Watch, MacBook, and Apple TV. Throughout the book, we will gradually introduce you to more and more programming concepts until we have enough knowledge to start creating our own programs. The book will let you create programs such as a small PokÃ©mon game, where PokÃ©mon will be able to battle each other.

We will also be creating an app to deliver pizzas in outer space and the aforementioned Movie Night app to keep a list of your favorite movies. After creating our programs, you will be able to install the applications on an iPhone and show it to your friends. After being introduced to Swift and the knowledge and tools required to create an application for the iPhone, you should be able to continue to explore this area of programming. You should not only be able to continue working on the applications we create throughout this book, but also be capable of continuing the learning journey using other books or Internet resources. By using the skills provided in this book along with some imagination, a lot of fun and useful applications can be created for iOS devices such as the iPhone.

Summary

In this chapter, we looked at what programming actually is, why it is useful, and examples of what we use programming for. We discussed what a world without programming would look like and we looked at a short introduction to the Swift programming language. Lastly, we introduced what the reader can expect to learn when reading this book and how this can be used moving further into the world of programming.

In the next chapter, we will go over the practical part of getting the user set up with the right tools in order to begin programming.

2
Getting Set Up

The first step in creating an application is getting yourself set up. This chapter helps you get set up by taking you through the necessary steps to install Xcode. We will also explain what Xcode and playgrounds are. These are essential tools in helping you learn how to code and create iOS applications. Think of it as the paint and the canvas an artist needs in order to paint a beautiful picture.

By the end of this chapter, you will have all the necessary tools that will allow you to begin your journey in creating an iOS application. In this chapter, we will cover:

- Downloading and installing Xcode
- Using Playground – for running Swift code

Xcode

If you were to send a text to a friend from your mobile phone, what steps would you take? What would you say? You would open up the messages application and write out a message to your friend telling them that you're learning how to code. After typing out your message on the screen, you think twice about adding a few pizza emojis to it. After sending the message, your mobile phone is able to interpret that information and send it over to your friend, all within a few seconds–how amazing!

 All related source code for this chapter can be found here: `https://githu b.com/swift-book-projects/swift-3-programming-for-kids/tree/ma ster/Chapter-2`

Powering the messages application that you're using to text your friend is code. This code is a list of instructions that is processed by a computer, written by developers like yourself. But where does a developer write code? It is written in an application that is known as an **Integrated Development Environment (IDE)**. An IDE is a piece of software that combines the basic tools developers need to write, test, and run their applications. Xcode is a specific IDE that includes everything you need to create amazing apps for iPhone, iPad, Mac, Apple Watch, and Apple TV. It is shown in the following screenshot:

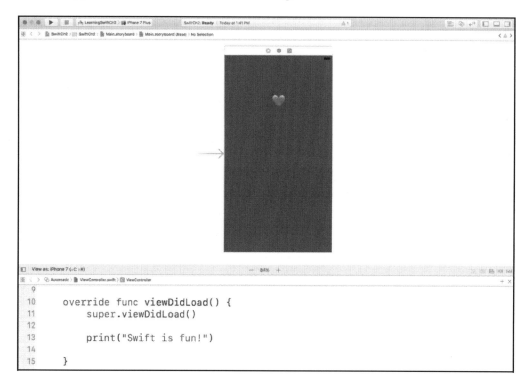

This is a screenshot of Xcode. We've begun working on an iOS app that displays a red heart on a blue background. After showing our friends how gorgeous our iOS app looks, one told us how we're going about it all wrong and that we should have a blue heart on a red background. Xcode allows us to easily make these changes:

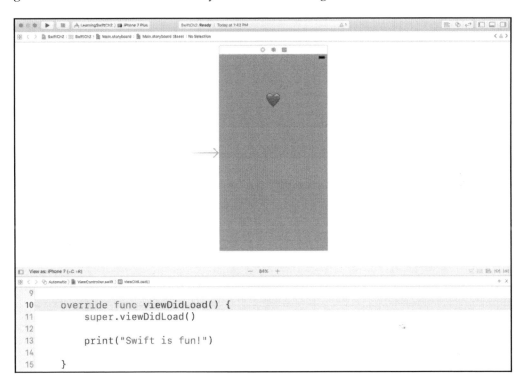

Downloading Xcode

In order for you to be able to install the latest version of Xcode (at the time of writing, it is version 8.2.1), you need to be on a Mac. You need to be running OS X 10.11.5 or later to install Xcode (at the time of writing).

The following are the instructions to download Xcode:

1. Open the **App Store** application on your Mac:

2. When in the **App Store** application, in the upper right-hand corner, search for Xcode, as illustrated:

3. Download Xcode; as of version 8.1, it's 4.47 GB:

Playground

After Xcode has finished installing, open the Finder application, which you should find on your toolbar (it looks like a smiling face). Within Finder, you should see that you have access to various directories. Select the applications directory, which should then list all of the available applications on your Mac. You should find Xcode in that list of applications. Considering, you might be working with Xcode a lot, you should drag this application down to your Dock for easy access. After doing so, launch Xcode.

After launching Xcode, you will be met with the following launch screen:

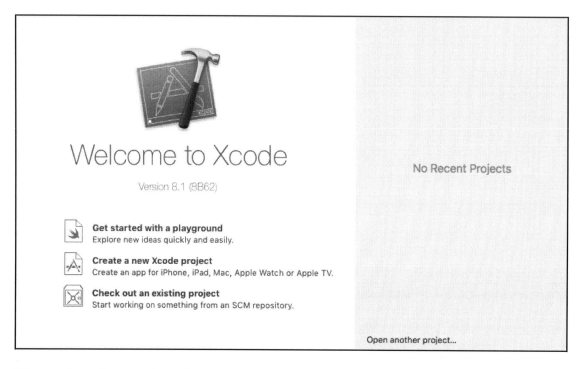

We are given three options. For now, we are most interested in **Get started with a playground**. Its description states, **Explore new ideas quickly and easily.** What exactly is a playground?

A playground is a place where we can write Swift code and see the results immediately. You won't be building apps in a playground, but they are a great place to learn:

Writing Swift code in a playground is very simple. As you're writing code, you will see the results in the right-hand pane, updated in real time, as illustrated:

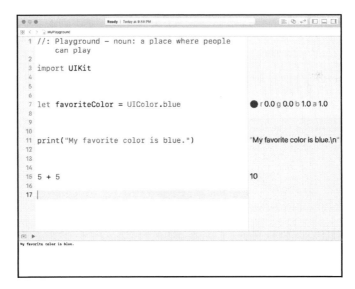

In subsequent chapters, you will be tasked with writing code in a playground file. This will make your learning experience more interactive. You will be able to see, in real time, whether or not your code (list of instructions) is doing what you expect.

You are now equipped with the necessary tools to begin your journey; We wish you luck!

Summary

In this chapter, we've set you up with the necessary tools to create iOS applications. In the next chapter, we will dive right in and write some Swift code, beginning with the most famous line of code ever.

```
print("Hello World")
```

Also, we will help you understand the various parts that make up Xcode and how you will interact with them when creating iOS applications.

3

Say Hello

For historic reasons, the first program we usually make when learning a new programming language is a program that simply outputs the text `Hello World` to the console. Printing to the console is reasonably simple and is, therefore, often a good starting point to ensure that everything is set up correctly. To honor traditions, we will do the same with our very first program written in the Swift programming language:

```
print("Hello World")
```

Exciting! To achieve this, the chapter will cover the following topics:

- Introducing a console application
- Setting up our first Xcode playground and taking a look at the most important parts of a playground
- Writing our first Hello World program using Swift and a playground
- A quick look at how Xcode playground communicates errors and how we can use autocompletion to write code faster and more safely

What is a console application?

You might be wondering what a console is. Before diving into writing the code, let's try to understand the difference between a **console** interface and a **Graphical User Interface** (**GUI**). We say that a console interface is an interface based on text. This means that we are able to interact with the interface using only text.

An application that uses a console interface can also be considered a console application. To understand what a console interface is like in practice, you can have a look at the interface of the Terminal application, which ships together with macOS:

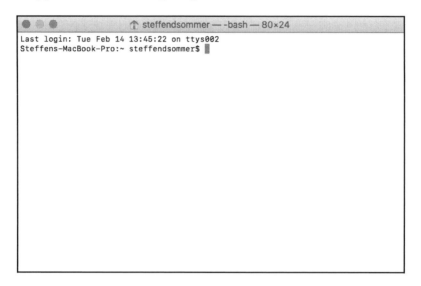

The Terminal application is a powerful application to control the underlying operating system. Everything is controlled by text in the sense that you write commands to instruct the operating system to do what you want. The output of your commands will be communicated back to you in text as well.

An iPhone is a great example of a device that uses a GUI. We are all very used to being able to click on icons to launch our applications, to swipe up and down to see our list scroll in an animated fashion, and to long press our icons to see them wiggle back and forth to indicate that you can move them. All this is often referred to as the **look and feel**, and it is all at the core of the concept of a GUI.

Setting up our first Xcode playground

With the release of Xcode 6, Apple introduced a new feature, called **playgrounds**. A playground is lightweight compared to a traditional Xcode project and is a great tool to try out things in Swift without having to worry about setting up a complete project. We can use a playground to write our first program, which will not have any GUI.

Creating the playground

Start off by opening up the Xcode application we installed in `Chapter 2`, *Getting Set Up*. Look for the following icon in your applications folder:

The first thing you will see in Xcode is the **Welcome to Xcode** window, which will give you quick access to creating new projects and opening your recent ones:

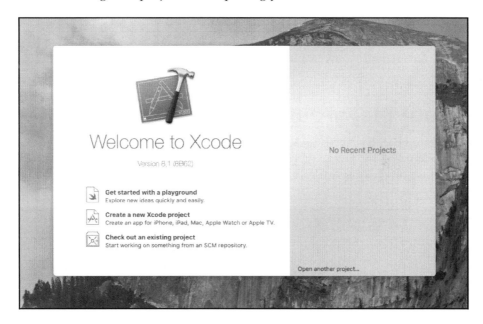

A complete application that can be installed, for example, on an iPhone, requires some project files and configuration. This is not needed now, as we just want to write our first line of Swift code, therefore, we will only focus on playgrounds. We will get back to how to set up a complete Xcode project in a later chapter.

Go ahead and click on the **Get started with a playground** item from the menu. Note that if you closed the **Welcome to Xcode** window, or it never appears for some reason, you can always create a new playground from the menu bar by navigating to **File** | **New** | **Playground...**, as illustrated:

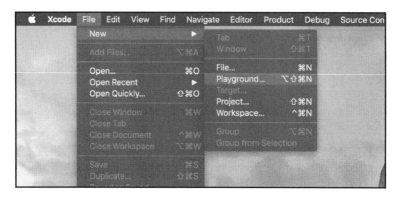

Now that we have created a new playground, let's move on to saving it.

Saving our playground

The next step is to enter a proper name for our new playground. We suggest typing in `HelloWorld` as a name for this playground. Next, we will choose the platform to target, which has the following three options:

- **iOS**: This is the platform for developing iPhone and iPad applications
- **macOS**: This is the platform for developing applications running on a Mac computer (for example, MacBook Pro)
- **tvOS**: This is the platform for developing Apple TV applications (requires Apple TV 4th generation or a later version at the time of writing)

A platform refers to the devices that should be able to run our application. As mentioned in Chapter 1, *What is Programming*, decisions on what programming language to use and what device to target are what set the boundaries in terms of the available functionality for our application:

After filling out the form and clicking on **Next**, a save dialog will appear. Go ahead and choose where to store your playground file:

Ensure that you remember where you save it so that you can always open it again if you want to continue exploring Swift in the playground. If you delete it, however, a new playground can always be created.

Removing what is unnecessary

Now we are getting really close to having our playground set up. Once you select where to save the playground file, the playground will automatically open, as illustrated:

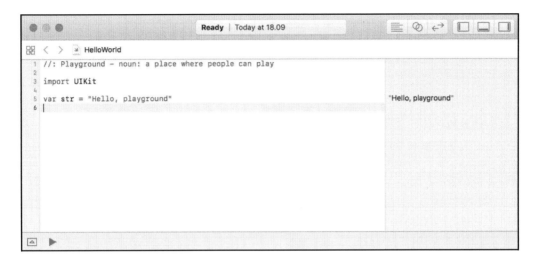

Don't worry about the content for now, as we won't be needing it. In fact, go ahead and remove all the text from the editor so that your playground is completely empty, as shown:

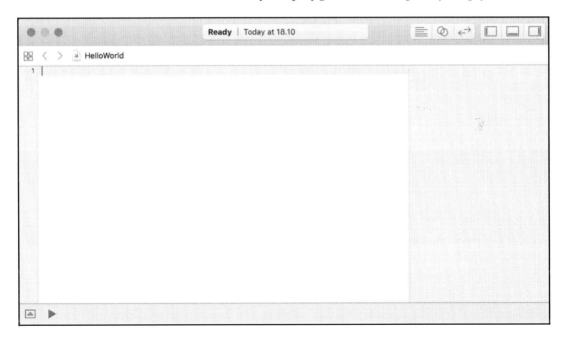

With our clean slate in place we are now ready to write our first lines of Swift code.

A quick look at the Xcode interface

By this time, we should have created our first playground file, saved it somewhere on our local drive, and deleted the autogenerated content in the editor. This means we now have a clean slate as our starting point.

Before writing our first line of Swift, let's quickly look at some of the interface elements of Xcode. For now, these are a few areas you should care about.

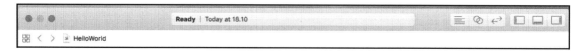

First up, we see the toolbar that sits at the top of the window. In the middle, we see the current status of our playground. When you first open up your playground, it might be doing some work before showing **Ready**. As soon as we make changes to our playground, that is, change or add some code in the editor, the status will change to **Running**, which means that Xcode is interpreting our instructions or recipe, as explained in Chapter 1, *What is Programming*. On the right-hand side of the toolbar, there are some buttons to show and hide different editors, navigators, and other areas of Xcode, which are currently hidden and which we don't need right now:

Below the toolbar, we have the actual editor. This is where we will be writing our Swift code. You might have noticed that the editor seems to be divided into two columns, where the column on the left has a white background color and the column on the right has a more gray color. The column on the left is the actual editor, where we are able to write our code. The column on the right is the result of running our playground (also called the **results sidebar**). This means that, if we want our program to output some text to the console, it will be shown in the right column. To give another example, if we programmed a small game, the actual game would be running on the right side.

At the bottom, there's a button to show/hide the console and a play button. If we click on the play button, we tell Xcode to run our application. In a playground, this will happen automatically as we write our code and save our playground. You might notice that when the status at the top says **Running**, the play button will change to a stop button, which can be used to tell Xcode to stop running our application.

The right column, which shows the results of our application, is what characterizes a playground in Xcode. Instead of running our application on an iPhone (or a simulator), we simply get a small area (in the column on the right) to preview the result of our code.

Creating our program

You might be wondering when we are supposed to actually start writing some Swift code; it is right now. Let's go straight to the code by typing the following code in the editor of our playground:

```
print("Hello World")
```

All related source code for this chapter can be found here: https://githu b.com/swift-book-projects/swift-3-programming-for-kids/tree/ma ster/Chapter-3

After writing this code in the editor, the playground should run. You can see this by checking whether the play button at the bottom changes to a stop button, or whether the status at the top shows **Running** instead of **Ready**. When the playground is done running, you should be able to see the result of our code in the right column. It should be as shown:

```
"Hello World\n"
```

Don't worry about \n being added to your print statement; it is simply Xcode adding it for our convenience. This sequence of characters (\n) will be translated into a new line when our application runs. This means that, if we add multiple print statements, Xcode ensures that they are shown on each of their own lines. Our playground should now look as follows:

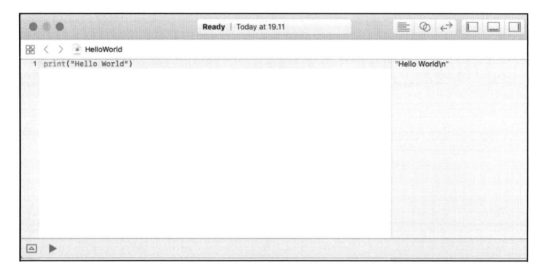

What exactly happened here? We used the word `print` to tell our application that we want to print something to the console. `print` is actually something called a **function**, which is why we use parentheses to enclose what we want to give to the function, but we will get back to that in a later chapter. Inside the parentheses, we indicate what we want to print in the console surrounded by double quotes, which is how we define a **string** in Swift. A string is basically a set of characters (letters, digits, and symbols); for example, the `Hello World` sentence.

How cool is that? Good job on writing your first line of Swift code! Actually, this is what programming is; you are doing it right now.

A quick look at Xcode errors

Let's continue with writing code by typing in the following line right after our current code:

```
print("We love Swift programming)
```

Uh oh, what happened? The playground is beginning to show red symbols in multiple places and we can't see our sentence in the results sidebar:

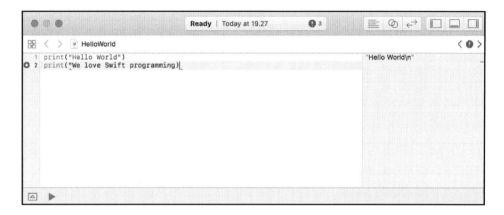

This is because we made an error and Xcode is now unable to understand the last piece of code we just added. This is normal in programming. We are only humans and, while experience and good software tools can help us, it is expected that we make a lot of errors while writing our code. Luckily for us, Xcode is helping us by letting us know which line we made an error on and, sometimes, Xcode will even be able to fix our errors. Can you spot the error? We forgot to finish our sentence by adding the double quote character ("). Go ahead and fix it by inserting the missing double quote and see if the error disappears. Great, now your playground should look like this:

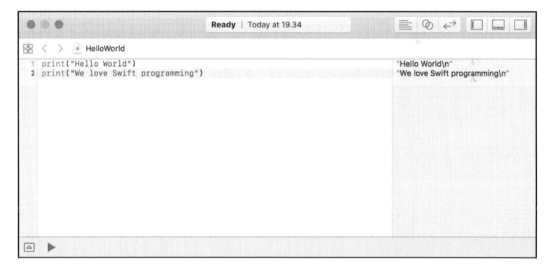

Good job, you now have two lines of Swift code running in your playground file without any errors. You are definitely off to a good start!

Xcode and autocompletion

You might have noticed a small window popping up while writing our first lines of Swift code. This is a feature called **autocompletion**. The idea of autocompletion is very similar to what we're used to when writing text messages on our iPhone. Before having written all the characters in a word, the messages app will suggest the word we're trying to write. This comes in handy since you save time by not typing all the characters in a word every single time.

Go to a new line and start writing the `pri` characters. Note how Xcode will show this small autocompletion window:

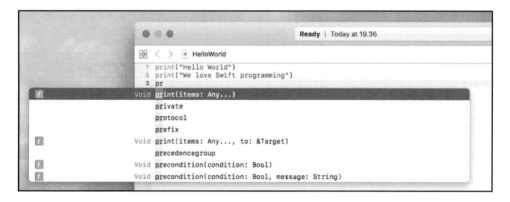

This is basically Xcode guessing what we're trying to do as we write. In this case, we want to add another `print` statement, so using the arrows on the keyboard to go up and down, we can select the correct instruction we want to perform. Select the proper instruction by pressing *Enter* and note how our playground looks:

The blue box inside the parentheses is something called a **placeholder**. This is basically telling us that we need to fill in something inside the parentheses. This makes sense because we want to print something. Let's write our favorite ice cream this time. Xcode will automatically select the placeholder, so you should be able to just start writing inside the parentheses. Start typing the `"My favourite ice cream is vanilla"` characters, and after writing these characters, pay attention to how the closing parenthesis is colored as compared to the other parentheses in our playground:

```
ming")
m is vanilla")
```

Do you note the difference? The last one seems to be more gray than black. This is because we haven't confirmed the autocompletion Xcode suggested. You can do this by pressing the *Tab* key, and the line of code should now be done.

Great job setting up your first playground and writing your first Swift code!

Summary

In this chapter, we introduced the notion of a console interface and a GUI. We saw how to create Xcode playgrounds and went over the most important parts of the playground interface. We looked at the common first program every new developer will probably create, which is printing Hello World in the console, and how this can be implemented using Swift and a playground. We quickly looked at how Xcode playgrounds communicate errors in our program and how to interpret them. Lastly, we looked at how Xcode offers something called autocompletion to help us write code in a faster and safer manner.

In the next chapter, we will cover a fundamental concept in programming–the use of variables and constants. These are very handy as they, for example, help us reference our favorite ice cream without having to write the complete name of the ice cream everywhere in our program.

4

Favorite Things

This chapter will introduce you to the concept of **variables** and **constants**. It will cover how we use them to manage state in an iOS application. We will take what you've learned in the last chapter in working with `print` statements and build upon that to help you understand the problem that is solved using variables and constants.

The topics this chapter covers are as follows:

- Creating variables and constants
- Assigning a value to a variable
- Reading a value from a variable

Variables and constants

What's your favorite Disney song? Our is *A Whole New World* from *Aladdin*. What's your favorite ice cream flavor? For us, nothing beats *vanilla*. If we wanted to print out some of our favorite items in a playground file, we know how to do that!

Create a new playground file and name it `FavoriteThings`, as illustrated. Save it wherever you like; we recommend saving all of this work in a place you can remember. That way, you can access it easily when you need to reference it later on:

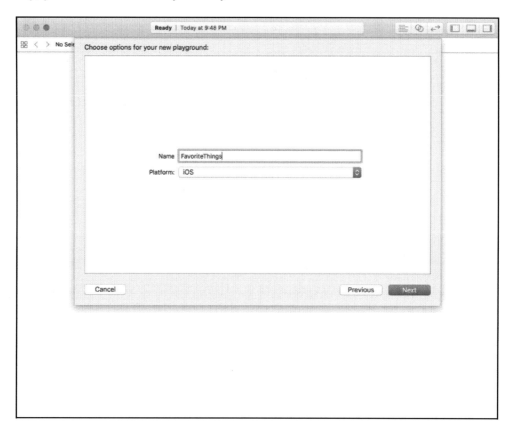

Clear out all the code that a newly created playground file provides to you; that way, you're left with a completely blank file:

We mentioned earlier that our favorite Disney song is *A Whole New World*. We also mentioned that our favorite ice cream flavor is *vanilla*. Let's pretend, for a second, that your best friend just asked you those questions. Instead of speaking to them, you decide to write some Swift code (because you're an awesome developer) and show them what prints to the console.

We can do this with the following lines of code:

```
print("My favorite Disney song is A Whole New World.")
print("My favorite ice-cream flavor is Vanilla")
```

 All related source code for this chapter can be found here: `https://githu b.com/swift-book-projects/swift-3-programming-for-kids/tree/ma ster/Chapter-4`

This is how your playground file should look if you're getting along:

Now, our best friend knows what our favorite Disney song and ice cream flavor is. A few days later, our favorite uncle asks us the exact same question. So, we create a new `print` statement letting uncle Carl know as we show off our new Swift skills:

```
print("Hi Uncle Carl, my favorite Disney song is A Whole New World. Also, my favorite ice-cream flavor is Vanilla")
```

Last but not least, our mother asks us the exact same question. So, we provide a `print` statement for her as well!

```
print("Hi Mom! <3 you. My favorite Disney song is A Whole New World. My favorite ice-cream flavor is Vanilla.")
```

As of now, your playground file should look like this:

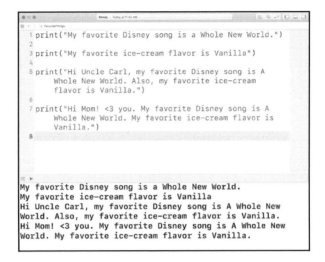

After feeling really proud about communicating to our friends and family through Swift code, our sister decides to burst our bubble. She takes a look at our application and asks us to change our favorite Disney song to *Let It Go*. Also, she asks us to change our favorite ice cream flavor to *strawberry*. After arguing about it for 30 minutes, we agree with her decision.

This leaves us with an annoying task. We now have to go through all of our code and manually change these items to reflect our new decision. So, let's do that.

On second thought, let's not do that. That's a lot of work, there has to be a better way. Is there a better way? Yes!

Variables

Imagine if we had the ability to store our favorite things in separate boxes (to help us remember). To help us organize and know what's inside each box, we will label them. If we want to find out what our favorite ice cream flavor is, we will go up to our boxes and look for the one labeled *Favorite Ice Cream*. After opening the box, we will see a piece of paper with the word *Vanilla* on it inside.

Can we do something like this in code? Yes, we can do it with variables. You can think of variables as containers (boxes) that hold information. Their sole purpose is to label and store information:

```
var favoriteIceCream = "Strawberry"
```

The preceding code is how we've created a new variable, called `favoriteIceCream` and gave it a value of `Strawberry`.

The variable `favoriteIceCream` represents our labeled box and `Strawberry` represents the piece of paper inside the box, letting us know what our favorite ice cream flavor is.

Here, `var` is what's known as a keyword. The `var` keyword being used here means variable. In order to create a variable in Swift, you have to preface the name of your variable with the `var` keyword. We've decided to call our variable `favoriteIceCream`. Why? This is because it's holding on to the value `Strawberry`. It represents what our favorite ice cream flavor is.

When you name your variables (label your boxes) in Swift, you should do so using the following technique. The first letter of your variable should *always* be lowercase. Every other word should be uppercase.

With this new found knowledge, try to create a new variable, called `favoriteDisneySong`, and give it a value of `Let It Go` without looking at the answer.

How did you do? Here's the answer:

```
var favoriteDisneySong = "Let It Go"
```

Arrange your playground file so that it looks like this:

```
var favoriteIceCream = "Strawberry"

var favoriteDisneySong = "Let It Go"

print("My favorite Disney song is a Whole New World.")

print("My favorite ice-cream flavor is Vanilla")

print("Hi Uncle Carl, my favorite Disney song is A
       Whole New World. Also, my favorite ice-cream
       flavor is Vanilla.")

print("Hi Mom! <3 you. My favorite Disney song is A
       Whole New World. My favorite ice-cream flavor is
       Vanilla.")
```
```
My favorite Disney song is a Whole New World.
My favorite ice-cream flavor is Vanilla
Hi Uncle Carl, my favorite Disney song is A Whole New
World. Also, my favorite ice-cream flavor is Vanilla.
Hi Mom! <3 you. My favorite Disney song is A Whole New
World. My favorite ice-cream flavor is Vanilla.
```

In the future chapters, we will discuss in detail as to what string interpolation is. For now, we will just use it–but first, we will give you a brief explanation as to what it is. String interpolation is the ability to replace any variable with its `String` value within the creation of another `String` value.

For example, if you replace the code on line 6 with the following, take a look at what is printed in the console:

Input:

```
print("My favorite Disney song is \(favoriteDisneySong)")
```

Output:

```
My favorite Disney song is Let It Go
```

Interesting! The code is able to open up our box labeled `favoriteDisneySong` and replace it with the string `Let It Go`. That's what is known as string interpolation. You have to add a back slash \ followed by two parentheses ( ). You have to put the name of your variable within these parentheses. Swift is then able to replace that variable with its value. The variable is `favoriteDisneySong` and its value is `Let It Go`.

Let's replace some of our code in the playground file to take advantage of using string interpolation. Before looking at the answer, see if you can replace all the places where you wrote out your favorite Disney song and your favorite ice cream with the variable instead:

```
1 var favoriteIceCream = "Strawberry"
2
3 var favoriteDisneySong = "Let It Go"
4
5 print("My favorite Disney song is \
      (favoriteDisneySong).")
6
7 print("My favorite ice-cream flavor is \
      (favoriteIceCream)")
8
9 print("Hi Uncle Carl, my favorite Disney song is \
      (favoriteDisneySong). Also, my favorite ice-cream
      flavor is \(favoriteIceCream).")
10
11 print("Hi Mom! <3 you. My favorite Disney song is \
      (favoriteDisneySong). My favorite ice-cream flavor
      is \(favoriteIceCream).")
12
```

```
My favorite ice-cream flavor is Strawberry
Hi Uncle Carl, my favorite Disney song is Let It Go. Also,
my favorite ice-cream flavor is Strawberry.
Hi Mom! <3 you. My favorite Disney song is Let It Go. My
favorite ice-cream flavor is Strawberry.
```

Look how easy it is now to change our favorite ice cream flavor and Disney song! We can change it in one place, and as soon as we make the change, our best friend, uncle Carl, and our mom are able to see the new results, without us having to manually change it everywhere.

Go ahead and try it some more! Change the variables to reflect your own favorite Disney song and ice cream flavor.

Constants

Create a new playground file and name it `Constants`. After doing so, clear all of its contents so that you're left with a blank slate.

Here's a quick challenge. Create a variable, called `favoriteColor`, and assign it a value that represents your favorite color. Our favorite color is green, so we will solve this problem as shown:

```
var favoriteColor = "Green"
```

On the next line, let's assign a different value to this `favoriteColor` variable:

```
favoriteColor = "Blue"
```

Your playground file should look something like this (depending on what colors you choose):

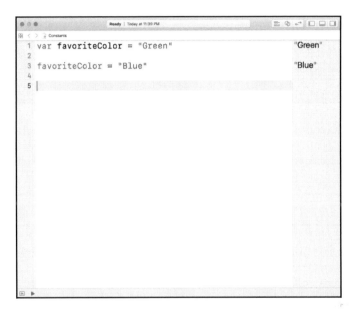

What if we were to print our `favoriteColor` variable. What would print out to the console? Let's try it out! Add this line of code where you changed the `favoriteColor` variable to `Blue`:

```
print(favoriteColor)
```

Well, look at that, `Blue` prints out to the console. This means we can change our variables throughout our application. The latest change that is made is the one that sticks:

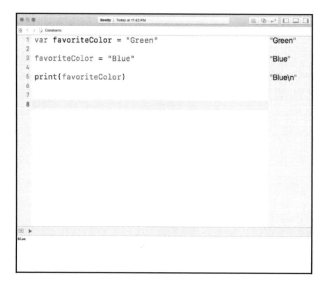

There will be times, though, when you will want to create a variable that should *never* be allowed to change. For instance, Jim's mother's name is `Maryann`. If we created a variable called `momsName`, we want to be able to assign it the value `Maryann` and ensure that it never changes. We can do this using what are known as constants in Swift. A constant is a variable that allows you to assign it a value only once!

```
let momsName = "Maryann"
```

The preceding code is how you create a constant, it's that simple! Can you spot the difference between creating a variable and creating a constant? The only difference is that we're using the `let` keyword instead of the `var` keyword. If we try assigning a new value to `momsName`, we will be met with an error. Let's try assigning the value `Patty` to our `momsName` constant to see the error Xcode produces:

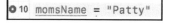

The code in the preceding screenshot is:

```
momsName = "Patty"
```

The error message that is provided is very informative:

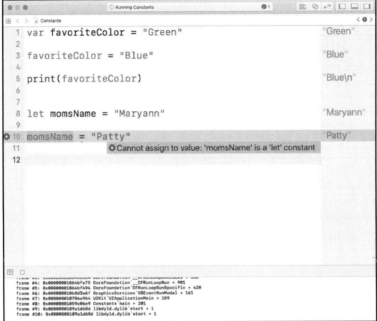

It's telling us that we can't assign a value to momsName because it's a let constant. That's great, it's exactly what we want! Throughout our entire application, momsName is guaranteed to have the value Maryann. There's no way that it can be any other value; this serves as a great tool and allows us to write very safe code.

Summary

In this chapter, you learned about an important building block that can be used with any application. We also looked at how to associate values with words that can be used throughout our application. These words are better known as variables. By learning what a variable is and how we can create them, we learned how to utilize a very important piece in creating an iOS application. Consider it your first major step!

Our next step, which will be covered in the next chapter, is learning what types are. In this chapter, we briefly went through what a String value looks like, but we will cover this topic in detail in subsequent chapters. We will cover what String means and how exactly we create String values.

5
Factories

This chapter will introduce you to the concept of types. A data type, or simply a type, is a classification of data. The type defines the operations that can be done on the data and the various attributes it might have. A sentence or a word can be considered as being a `String`. A number (non-decimal) can be considered to be an `Int` type. We will cover what exactly `String` and `Int` are along with how to create our own instances of `String` and `Int`. An instance is the actual number or the actual word we're referring to.

In this chapter, we will cover the following topics:

- Creating an instance of a `String`, `Int`, and `Double`
- Having a clear understanding as to what a type is

String and Int

There are only a few things on this Earth that are better than ice cream. we're just having trouble naming them. How is ice cream actually made? Well, it is made in an ice cream factory. This factory is able to create different flavors and toppings.

What about cars, how are cars made? Similar to ice cream, a car is made in a car factory. A car factory can create all kinds of different cars that we can drive around.

In Swift, there are many factories built into the language that are available for us to use. However, Swift doesn't refer to them as factories, it refers to them as **types**.

When a car factory creates a car, the car that is now in your possession is referred to as an **instance** of car (in Swift, types begin with an uppercase letter). Having your own instance of a car is like having a car in your driveway that you're able to use whenever you want, it's yours! You could drive it, park it, change its color, turn left, turn right, and play music. All of these actions are referred to as **functions** in Swift. Functions are actions that you can perform with instances of types.

Swift has different types that we can create instances of, which will help us create awesome applications.

The first type that we will talk about is the `String` type. Again, think of the `String` type as a factory that can create instances of `String` for us to use in our app. What does an instance of `String` actually look like? The following are three examples of `String` instances:

```
"Hello World"
"Frodo is the best hobbit!"
"I'm so hungry, I can eat an entire pizza."
```

You've been working with instances of `String` all along and you didn't even know it! Lets take this a step further:

```
let favoriteColor = "Blue"
```

All related source code for this chapter can be found here: `https://githu b.com/swift-book-projects/swift-3-programming-for-kids/tree/ma ster/Chapter-5`

This is code that you've seen before. In fact, you've written code just like this already! We just learned, in the last chapter, that variables and constants store values. It means that wherever we use `favoriteColor` in our code, we're actually referring to the value `Blue` because it's storing this value for us wherever it goes. Every value in Swift is an instance of some type. Now, knowing this, what would you guess is the type of `favoriteColor`.

The `favoriteColor` constant is of the `String` type. To confirm this, while holding down the *option* key on your keyboard, we will select the `favoriteColor` constant in our playground file to be met with the following tooltip:

```
10  let favoriteColor = "Blue"

Declaration   let favoriteColor: String
Declared In   Types.playground
```

Note what's to the right of the word **Declaration–let favoriteColor: String**.

This can be read like so: here we've declared a constant, called `favoriteColor`, of the `String` type. Anytime you see a colon (`:`), it can be replaced with the words *of type*.

How did Swift know that `favoriteColor` was of the `String` type. We didn't specify that it was of the `String` type, we just typed out some characters within double quotes. That's precisely how Swift was able to figure out that it was an instance of `String`. This process is known as **type inference**. Surrounding characters in double quotes is formally known as a **string literal** and when Swift sees this code, it's able to immediately tell that it's a `String` and properly label the variable or constant as being of that type.

Here are some more examples of using type inference in Swift to create some variables:

```
let name = "Jim"
let catName = "Hanna"
var favoriteFood = "Pasta"
```

We've created a constant, called `name`, of the `String` type, assigning it the value `Jim`. We've also created a constant, called `catName`, of the `String` type, assigning it the value `Hanna`. Lastly, we've created a variable, called `favoriteFood`, of the `String` type, assigning it the value `Pasta`.

Can you create instances of `String` without using type inference? Yes.

Instead of taking advantage of type inference in your creation of a variable or constant, you can be explicit with the type information, as shown:

```
let momsName: String = "Maryann"
```

Here, we've created a constant, called `momsName`, of the `String` type, assigning it the value `Maryann`. If we were to hold the *option* key and click on the `momsName` constant, we would also see that it's of the `String` type:

This comes in very handy when you're looking to create a variable that will ultimately store a value for you that you don't need immediately. What does that mean?

Imagine that you're creating an app that will ask everyone in your family what they want to eat for dinner. You might create the following constant:

```
let question = "What do you want to eat for dinner?"
```

Where will we store the answer? Let's create a variable that will store their response:

```
var answer: String
```

`answer` is a variable of the `String` type. However, you might have noted that we haven't yet assigned it a value. You may say that it's valueless, that is, it doesn't have *any* value at declaration. If we try to use this `answer` variable before assigning it a value, our application will crash.

Let's see that in action; we will attempt to print the answer variable only to be met with a crash in our playground:

The error states that the `answer` variable is used before being initialized. If we want to get rid of this error, we need to assign a value to this `answer` variable. Let's pretend that our sister gave us a response, which we can now store in this variable. we will assign the value `Cake` to the `answer` variable because, of course, that's what she wants to eat for dinner:

This is pretty neat. What happened here is that the compiler is making sure that we have values assigned to our constants or variables before we use them. Variables or constants must have their types known at declaration but don't need to have an initial value (as we did earlier). This is one of the many fundamental building blocks that will allow us to build versatile applications in Swift.

So far, we've only dealt with one type–the `String` type. However, if we lived in a world where there was only an ice cream factory producing ice cream, we would get very sick (although we would still want to live in that world). There are different kinds of factories producing all sorts of things that we can use in our day-to-day life; the same can be said for Swift. If we want a donut, we won't walk up to the ice cream factory, we will go to the donut factory.

In Swift, if you want a number, there are different types (or factories) that we can utilize to create the type of number we want.

You can easily create numbers in Swift as follows:

```
var age = 75
```

In creating this `age` variable, we've assigned it the value `75`. Note how there aren't any double quotes around `75`. If there were, it would instead be of the `String` type. Writing out a number as shown by itself (with no double quotes) is producing a number, not a `String`. So, if we were to hold down the *option* key and click on the age variable, what would be its type?

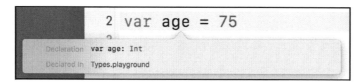

It's of the `Int` type. As it's an `Int` (short for integer), we can perform math operations on it, unlike a `String`:

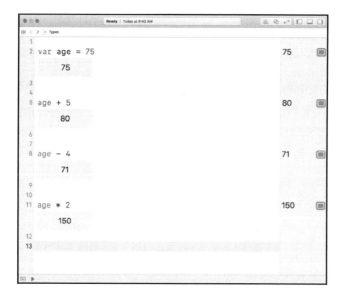

We've included the result of the math operation as follows. Let's walk through the first one, `age + 5` . Note how `age` is a variable of the `Int` type. It's represented by its value (which is `75`). The mathematical operation of `age + 5` can be broken down as `75 + 5` (because you replace your variable or constant with its value).

You might have noted that we're taking advantage of type inference again. Swift is able to figure out the type we intend to use without us having to be explicit about it. However, similar to creating `String`, we can be explicit if we want to:

```
var hitPoints: Int = 95
let planetsInSolarSystem: Int = 8
```

`hitPoints` is a variable of the `Int` type with a value of `95`. `planetsInSolarSystem` is a constant of the `Int` type with a value of `8`.

Double

Swift has a different type (or factory) for creating decimals (numbers that aren't whole numbers):

```
let temperatureInF = 85.2
```

The `temperatureInF` constant is of the `Double` type. To confirm this, while holding down the *option* key on our keyboard, we will select the `temperatureInF` constant in our playground file to be met with the following tooltip:

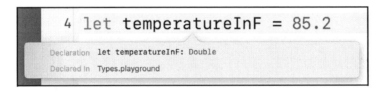

Swift, again using type inference, is doing this for us. We can just as easily be explicit about the type of our variable or constant at declaration, as follows:

```
let heightInCM: Double = 187.96
```

We've created a constant, called `heightInCM`, of the `Double` type and assigned it a value of `187.96`.

You now retain the fundamental building blocks of every application you've ever used. There are various types that we utilize when writing code; these separate types have their own distinct set of functions. Controlling the interaction of all these types in our code through the use of functions is what powers an application.

In the next chapter, you will learn what a function is in more detail. To help you out, think of a function as an action that can be performed. If you had an instance of a car, you can call (or perform) functions that are available only to cars on it. `drive` is a function that, when called, will make our car move forward. `turnLeft` is a function that will make our car turn left. `park` is another function that will make our car stop moving.

Summary

The three types we learned about in this chapter were `String`, `Int`, and `Double`. In the subsequent chapters, we will introduce you to many more types.

Now that we have an understanding as to what a type is, in the next chapter, we will introduce you to functions. Functions can be summed up as actions that can be performed in your code. A car can turn right or left and these can be considered actions (or functions) that you perform on a car. Functions are self-contained chunks of code that you can think of as actions. We will cover what functions are and how to call them in the next chapter.

6

Making Pizza

Until now, we have been looking at how to create certain types and how to use variables as a tool for representing values in our programs. These are all fundamental concepts to understand when learning how to program, and this chapter will build upon that. In this chapter, we will take a look at something called **functions**.

As you have learned from Chapter 4, *Favorite Things*, a variable can represent a value in our program. This means that without knowing the actual value, we can use the variable throughout our program to represent that value. In a way, you could say that we are *reusing* the value throughout the program by just using our variable. A function shares similar advantages in the sense that we are also reusing code when we use a function. We say that a function abstracts an amount of work we only have to define once. This idea of reusing code is central to programming and functions are just a tool to help programmers do that.

In this chapter, the reader will learn the following things:

- How the iPhone (or most computers) understands our recipe–our program
- How a program could look without using the concept of functions
- What a function is, including how to visualize a function and what it looks like in Swift
- How to create one's own functions using Swift

How the iPhone runs our program

To understand what a function is and how it works, it makes sense to first have a look at how a computer, let's say the iPhone, understands or runs our program. Remember from Chapter 1, *What is Programming?*, that we can think of the code in our program as a recipe for the iPhone to interpret in order to know how our application should work. The way that an iPhone will read our recipe is to go through it line by line, beginning from the top and moving to the bottom, just as we would normally do with a text, book, or recipe. Maybe you already noted it in our earlier playgrounds that anything we print to the console will be printed in the same order as Xcode reads our code, line by line, from the source editor.

To make it clear, let's revisit our playground from Chapter 3, *Say Hello*. This was how we left it:

```
print("Hello World")
print("We love Swift programming")
print("My favorite ice cream is vanilla")
```

If you click on the small button with an arrow pointing upwards, you will bring up the console, also called the **debug area**:

The debug area should not be confused with the sidebar area, which is the column on the right in Xcode, also showing the same text being printed. The difference is that the result sidebar is there to show basically any result of our program. If we decided to show an image of a dragon, this would show up in the result sidebar. The console, however, is limited to only showing any text that we might want to output:

Hello World
We love Swift programming
My favourite ice cream is vanilla

If you click on the button to show the debug area, you should be able to see the following output in your console:

```
Hello World
We love Swift programming
My favorite ice cream is vanilla
```

Note how Hello World is being printed as the first thing in our console. This is because we asked our program to do this on line 1 of our application:

```
print("Hello World")
```

This confirms that Xcode will read our program line by line, starting from the top.

A simple program without functions

Having an understanding of how our iPhone reads our code as a line by line recipe can help us understand the need for the concept of a function.

Let's imagine, for a moment, that we do not have any concept of functions when writing our code. Then, if we want to make a simple app that simulates the making of a pizza, we can write the following code:

```
print("Flattening the dough to form a round pizza 🤚")
print("Adding some tomato sauce 🍅")
print("Adding some mozzarella cheese 🧀")
print("Adding some spicy pepperoni 🍕")
print("Preparing the pizza in the oven ♨️")
print("Done! Delicious pizza ready to be eaten 🍴")
```

 All related source code for this chapter can be found here: `https://githu
b.com/swift-book-projects/swift-3-programming-for-kids/tree/ma
ster/Chapter-6`

When we run this application, it will simply output the simulation of making a pizza to the console:

How will we write our code if we want our program to make multiple pizzas? The first thing that comes to mind is to repeat our code for each pizza that needs to be made:

```
print("Flattening the dough to form a round pizza 🖐")
print("Adding some tomato sauce 🍅")
print("Adding some mozzarella cheese 🧀")
print("Adding some spicy pepperoni 🍕")
print("Preparing the pizza in the oven ♨")
print("Done! Delicious pizza ready to be eaten 🍴")

print("Flattening the dough to form a round pizza 🖐")
print("Adding some tomato sauce 🍅")
print("Adding some mozzarella cheese 🧀")
print("Adding some spicy pepperoni 🍕")
print("Preparing the pizza in the oven ♨")
print("Done! Delicious pizza ready to be eaten 🍴")

print("Flattening the dough to form a round pizza 🖐")
print("Adding some tomato sauce 🍅")
print("Adding some mozzarella cheese 🧀")
print("Adding some spicy pepperoni 🍕")
print("Preparing the pizza in the oven ♨")
print("Done! Delicious pizza ready to be eaten 🍴")
```

In the preceding program, we're simulating that we're making three pizzas. If we want the ingredients on our pizzas to be different, we can now change it for each pizza and our program would then be able to make different pizzas when we run it.

When we look at the preceding code, it becomes clear that something can be improved. You might have noted how repetitive our code is. Having to be repetitive takes up a lot of lines of code, which can make it more difficult to understand, specially if we imagine applications that have thousands of lines of source code. It also doesn't scale very well. Let's say, instead of making three pizzas, we want to make 25 or 100 pizzas; then it starts becoming messy and harder to grasp. If you are working with a friend on an application, improving the code, will be easier for others, and to understand your code. Otherwise, you will end up spending a lot of time explaining how the code works. Also, if you paused working on your application for a couple of months and then decided to work on it again, it quickly becomes difficult to remember where you left it. If you don't think about writing code that is easy to understand and maintain, then you will end up spending a lot of time and mental energy on trying to understand your code. In our pizza application, one can say that it becomes more difficult to understand how our program works with each repetition we make.

Consider the following line in our code:

```
print("Adding some spicy pepperoni 🍕")
```

What if want to use the 🍕 emoji instead of 🍕 to help illustrate that our program is putting pepperoni on our pizza? With our current program, we will have to go through our code and change it in three places because we're currently making three pizzas with pepperoni. As you can imagine, this becomes more difficult when the number of lines in our code grows; this is an example of why programmers want to avoid repetition.

What is a function?

Going back to `Chapter 1`, *What is Programming?*, you may remember that we defined programming as writing a set of instructions for a computer to execute. A function is a block of reusable code or instructions which generally performs a single specific task. A function abstracts one or more instructions and gives us a reference to that block of instructions. `Chapter 4`, *Favorite Things*, showed us how to reference values using variables. In this chapter, you will learn that a function is basically a set of instructions or a chunk of code that is grouped together and referenced by a function name.

Let's imagine a real-world example for a moment. When you want to order a pizza, you call your local pizza joint. The people working at the pizza joint will then note down your order, put it into their queue of orders, make the pizza specified in your order and lastly, have it delivered to your address.

Actually, we can model these tasks as multiple functions:

- A function to receive the order from the customer
- A function to find the next order in the queue of orders
- A function to make the actual pizza
- A function to deliver the pizza to the customer

To help visualize what a function is, we can think of it as being a person performing a specific task–a person working at the pizza joint who writes down the order when we call them; a person who finds the next order in the queue; a person who takes the order and makes the pizza; and finally, a person who grabs the pizza and delivers it to you. We can think of a function being a person responsible for one specific task that we can ask the person to perform. We might need to give the person some information related to the task, for example, the pizza we want to order, and the person might return something after the task has been performed, for example, the pizza.

This series of work performed at the pizza joint–taking the order, putting it into the order queue, and finally, making the pizza–has some shared characteristics with a function in a programming language, such as Swift.

A function can receive some input

When we want to order a pizza at our local pizza joint, we usually call the place and let them know what pizza on the menu we want to order. If we imagine the person working at the pizza joint to be our function, we could say that the pizza we want to order is the input for that function. If the pizza joint is expecting multiple input, for example, my order and my phone number, the order of which I provide the input is important. We can generally think of input as being the information needed to perform the task the function is responsible for. Similarly, one can think of devices such as a keyboard, mouse, trackpad, and more being input for a computer:

These devices help us communicate with our computer in terms of input which the computer can process and then, for example, display it on a computer monitor.

A function can be pure

A function can be self-contained (or pure), which means that all the requirements needed in order for a function to perform its task are provided to the function. If we take a look at the arithmetic operation of addition, that is, adding two numbers together, for example, $2 + 3 = 5$, we can consider this operation as a function. The function takes in two or more input values, in this case the values 2 and 3, and it returns the result of the operation, in this case 5. When moving a shipping container around the world, the container is filled with the goods it is supposed to carry and then locked. The container does not magically get more goods after being locked and made ready for transportation. Its function to carry goods is literally self-contained.

Going back to our pizza example, we can say that in order for the pizza joint to process our order, they obviously need some input. They need to know what pizza we want and we can inform them using a name or number from their menu. We don't call the pizza joint saying that we want a pizza and then hang up, expecting that they will call us back for more information when they start making the pizza. In this case, we could say that the task of making our pizza is self-contained because all the information needed in order to make the pizza is given upfront before performing the task.

A function can return something

When we ask a person to perform a task, there might be a result that is being returned to us after the task has been performed. In our pizza example, we can consider the actual pizza being the result of the pizza joint or the chef performing the task of making our pizza. In the example, with the arithmetic operation, the result of adding 2 and 3 is the result or the return value of that task. A person delivering ordered goods is like a function returning a value to its caller:

There might be cases where a function or task does not return anything. It might be that we're not interested in the result, but it could also be the case where the task does not generate any result at all. Let's revisit some of the code we created together in Chapter 3, *Say Hello*:

```
print("Hello World")
```

As we learned in Chapter 3, *Say Hello*, this simple piece of code does nothing other than print Hello World to the console. What if we abstracted this work of printing the sentence, which means that we would be able to call a function that takes care of printing the sentence to the console. What would the return value be? The sentence itself or maybe nothing? Sometimes it does not make sense to return a value, and having a function that only prints to the console is a reasonable example. We can refer to these functions as *fire and forget* functions as we call them, but without knowing what happens next, in the sense that we don't get a response indicating whether they succeeded or not.

A look at functions in Swift

We've been covering some of the different characteristics of functions that are shared among different programming languages. Next, let's focus on what functions in Swift look like.

Let's start by creating the function that simply prints `Hello World` to the console. This function does not take any input values and it will not return any value:

```
func sayHello() {
    print("Hello World")
}
```

We declare a function using the `func` keyword. This is how Swift has defined what a function looks like and this ensures that our iPhone will know that this is a function. The next part is the name of our function, in this case `sayHello`. In Swift, we define our function names using a strategy, called **camel case**. It is a simple pattern where we write names with no spaces or hyphens but capitalize each word or abbreviation in the middle of the phrase. Camel case can start with a capital letter or a lowercase letter. In Swift, we use a lowercase letter for the first word in our methods. The next part of our function is the parentheses– `()`. The parentheses contains the input values for our function. If we're not interested in any input values, we omit them by making the parentheses empty, as in our current example. The last part is our function body, which is indicated by our curly braces–`{ }`. The code we place inside our function body will be executed when we call our function. We say that we call or invoke our function when referencing the function name with zero or many input values. Input values are usually referred to as `parameters` and we say that a function takes *x* parameters. Parameters are usually denoted by a label, which are basically variables for the function. This means that when we call a function with some values, these values are assigned to the variables (or labels) of the function. This is convenient as we can then access these values inside the function body.

Before creating our own function and looking at how we can call them, let's take a quick look at a couple of examples of what functions look like in Swift. The following one takes in a parameter that is the `text` and it has to be of the `String` type. The function doesn't return any value and all it does is to print the specified `text` value to the console:

```
func printToConsole(text: String) {
    print(text)
}
```

The next function takes in two parameters: `firstName` and `lastName`. This function returns a value, as indicated by `->` (and the `return` statement inside the function body) and the type of the return value is `String`. The function body creates a string using the specified `firstName` and `lastName` and returns it:

```
func fullName(firstName: String, lastName: String) -> String {
    let fullName = "\(firstName) \(lastName)"
    return fullName
}
```

Making our own function

Earlier in the chapter, we looked at how one could write code that simulates the making of a pizza. The code looked like this:

```
print("Flattening the dough to form a round pizza 👆")
print("Adding some tomato sauce 🍅")
print("Adding some mozzarella cheese 🧀")
print("Adding some spicy pepperoni 🍕")
print("Preparing the pizza in the oven ♨")
print("Done! Delicious pizza ready to be eaten 🍴")
```

We discussed how this will scale if one would like to make many pizzas and the issues associated with that. Let's now look at how we can solve this by abstracting the preceding code using a function.

Go ahead and create a new Xcode playground and type in the preceding code:

The first thing we can do is to move our lines of code into a function body. Let's name our function `makePizza` for now. The function shouldn't take in any parameters and it will not return anything:

```
func makePizza() {
    print("Flattening the dough to form a round pizza 🤚")
    print("Adding some tomato sauce 🍅")
    print("Adding some mozzarella cheese 🧀")
    print("Adding some spicy pepperoni 🍕")
    print("Preparing the pizza in the oven ♨️")
    print("Done! Delicious pizza ready to be eaten 🍴")
}
```

To call this function, all we need to do is reference the function by its name, `makePizza()`, outside the function body. You should have the following code in your playground at this point:

Recall how Xcode runs our program, line by line from the top to the bottom of our playground; using functions breaks this pattern. In fact, our code for creating our pizza is not run before our function is called. This can quickly be verified by removing the call to our function (`makePizza()`) and see that nothing is printed to the console. Basically, the code inside a function body will not be run by Xcode before the function is called.

Let's iterate on our function by adding some parameters to specify the type of ingredients for our pizza and also, let's make it return the pizza in the form of a string describing our pizza. Most pizzas have tomato sauce and mozzarella cheese on them, but they can differ a lot in the rest of the ingredients; let's accommodate this by specifying all the ingredients besides tomato sauce and mozzarella cheese in a parameter to our function:

```
func makePizza(ingredients: String) -> String {
    print("Flattening the dough to form a round pizza 👋")
    print("Adding some tomato sauce 🍅")
    print("Adding some mozzarella cheese 🧀")
    print("Adding some \(ingredients)")
    print("Preparing the pizza in the oven ♨")
    print("Done! Delicious pizza ready to be eaten 🍴")
    return "Pizza with \(ingredients)"
}
```

Now that our function takes in a parameter and returns a value of the String type, we need to change the way we call our function. At the same time, because our function now returns a value, we can assign that value to a constant:

```
let myPizza = makePizza(ingredients: "meatballs 🍖")
```

If we take a look at the console, we can see that the pizza being made is using the ingredients we specified in the function call:

With our pizza-making function, it is now very easy to make multiple pizzas:

```
let pizzaWithMeatballs = makePizza(ingredients: "meatballs 🍖")
let pizzaWithSlicedHam = makePizza(ingredients: "sliced ham 🐖")
let pizzaWithShrimps = makePizza(ingredients: "shrimps 🍤")
```

Note, how we managed to remove a lot of duplicate code compared to what we did earlier in this chapter. We now have a centralized place for making a pizza, and any changes to that only need to be done once. Further, we have a way of making pizzas with different ingredients without having to change the fundamentals of a pizza being made.

The return value of our function makes it possible for us to store the different pizzas for later references in our code. In fact, suppose we print our different pizzas to the console, as shown:

```
print(pizzaWithMeatballs)
print(pizzaWithSlicedHam)
print(pizzaWithShrimps)
```

We should see something like this at the bottom of our console as a result:

Summary

In this chapter, we looked at how Xcode runs our playground and what a program can look like without the concept of functions. The concept of functions was introduced on a metaphorical level with tips on how one can visualize a function, with three common characteristics of a function being the following:

- It can receive some input
- It can be pure
- It can return something

Further, we looked at different examples of functions written in Swift before creating our own function for simulating the task of creating a pizza.

In the next chapter, we will explore new and exciting concepts of programming, such as arrays and dictionaries, which are useful for storing our values in boxes.

7
Toy Bin

When creating your application, there might come a point where you need to create a list, or you might come to a point where you want to associate a bunch of values with a bunch of other values (like a real-life dictionary). To solve this problem, we will walk you through what an array is and what a dictionary is in this chapter. These are considered collection types in Swift and are very powerful.

This chapter will help you understand the following things:

- An **array** is a collection type that allows you to store an ordered list of values
- A **dictionary** is a collection type that is unordered and associates various keys with values
- An **optional** is a type that handles the situation where there might not be a value

Collection types

All year, you've been dreaming of finally taking that family vacation to the moon.
Marisa (your neighbor) went last year and it's all she ever talks about. After begging your
parents to take you and your sister to the moon for a family vacation, you awoke to see this
note slipped through your door.

Yes! We're going to the moon. On second thoughts, now that we're finally going, it does
sound a little scary to be leaving everything behind for a full month. Also, we need to reply
by writing Swift code, that doesn't seem too bad.

In the earlier chapters, we've learned that there are various types built into the Swift
language:

```
let name = "Jim"
let age = 21
```

Here, `name` is a constant of the `String` type and `age` is a constant of the `Int` type. They
have both been assigned values: `name` has been assigned the value `Jim` and `age` has been
assigned the value `21`. Let's get back to the note we received now. It's asking us to create a
list. What we need to do is generate a list of values, so how do we do that in Swift?

Before we get into that, let's come up with the list of toys we want to take with us:

- Legos
- Dungeons and dragons
- Gameboy
- Monopoly
- Rubix cube

Now that we have our list, how can we generate this list in Swift?

Array

An array stores values of the same type in an ordered list. Below is an example of an array:

```
let list = ["Legos", "Dungeons and Dragons", "Gameboy", "Monopoly", "Rubix
Cube"]
```

All related source code for this chapter can be found here: https://githu
b.com/swift-book-projects/swift-3-programming-for-kids/tree/ma
ster/Chapter-7

This is an **array** (which you can think of as a list). Arrays are an ordered collection of values.

We've created a constant called `list` of the `[String]` type and assigned it a value that represents our list of toys that we want to take with us. When describing arrays, you surround the type of the values that are being stored in the array by square brackets, `[String]`. The following is another array called numbers, which contains four values, being 5, 2, 9 and 22:

```
let numbers = [5, 2, 9, 22]
```

You would describe `numbers` as being an array which contains `Int` values, which can be written as `[Int]`. We can confirm this by holding *Alt* and selecting the `numbers` constant to see what its type is in a playground file:

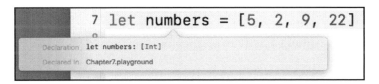

What if we were to go back and confirm that `list` is an array of `String` values. Let's *Alt* click that constant to make sure:

```
4 let list = ["Legos", "Dungeons and Dragons", "Gameboy",
   "Monopoly" "Rubix Cube"]
   Declaration  let list: [String]
   Declared In  Chapter7.playground
```

Similar to how we created instances of `String` and `Int` in earlier chapters without providing any type information, we're doing the same thing here when we create `list` and `numbers`. Both `list` and `numbers` are created by taking advantage of type inference. In creating our two arrays, we weren't explicit in providing any type information, we just created the array and Swift was able to figure out the type of the array for us.

If we want to, though, we can provide type information, as follows:

```
let colors: [String] = ["Red", "Orange", "Yellow"]
```

`colors` is a constant of the `[String]` type.

Now that we know how to create an array in Swift which can be compared to a list in real life, how can we actually use it? Can we access various items from the array? If so, how? Also, can we add new items to the list in case we forgot to include any items? Yes to all of these questions.

Every element (or item) in an array is indexed. What does that mean? Well, you can think of being indexed as being numbered. Except that there's one big difference between how we humans number things and how arrays number things. Humans start from 1 when they create a list (just like we did when we created our preceding list). An array starts from 0. So, the first element in an array is considered to be at index 0:

Always remember that the first item in any array begins at 0. This means that the index is used as an offset. The first element of the array is exactly contained in a location that the array refers to (being 0 elements away from this location).

If we want to grab the first item from an array, we will do so as shown, using what is referred to as subscript syntax:

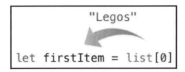

That 0 enclosed in two square brackets is what is known as subscript syntax. We are looking to access a certain element in the array at a certain index. In order to do that, we need to use subscript index, including the index of the item we want within square brackets. In doing so, it will return the value at the index. The value at the index in our preceding example is Legos. The = sign is also referred to as the assignment operator. So, we are assigning the Legos value to a new constant, called firstItem.

If we were to print out firstItem, Legos should print to the console:

```
print(firstItem)
// Prints "Legos"
```

If we want to grab the last item in this array, how do we do it?

Well, there are five items in the array, so the last item should be at index 5, right? Wrong!

What if we wrote the following code (which would be incorrect!):

```
let lastItem = list[5]
```

This would crash our application, which would be bad. When working with arrays, you need to ensure that you don't attempt to grab an item at an index that doesn't exist. There is no item in our array at index 5, which would make our application crash. When you run your app, you will receive the fatal error: Index out of range error. This is shown in the following screenshot:

```
  9  let lastItem = list[5]
 10     error: Execution was interrupted, reason: EXC_BAD_INSTRUCTION
```

Let's correctly grab the last item in the array:

```
let lastItem = list[4]

print("I'm not as good as my sister, but I love solving the \(lastItem)")
// Prints "I'm not as good as my sister, but I love solving the Rubix Cube"
```

Comments in code are made by writing text after //. None of this text will be considered code and will not be executed; it's a way for you to leave notes in your code.

Note that because arrays start with an index of 0, that this means that the index of the last element is `lastItem.count - 1`.

All of a sudden, you've now decided that you don't want to take the rubix cube as it's too difficult to play with. You were never able to solve it on Earth, so you start wondering why bringing it to the moon would help solve that problem. Bringing crayons is a much better idea.

Let's swap out the `Rubix cube` for `Crayons`. But how do we do that?

Using subscript syntax, we should be able to assign a new value to the array. Let's give it a shot:

```
list[4] = "Crayons"
```

This will not work! But why? Can you take a guess?

```
11  list[4] = "Crayons"
12                        Cannot assign through subscript: 'list' is a 'let' constant
```

It's telling us that we cannot assign through subscript because `list` is a constant (we declared it using the `let` keyword). Ah! That's exactly how `String` and `Int` work. We decide whether or not we can change (mutate) the array based upon the `let` or `var` keyword just like every other type in Swift. Let's change the list array to a variable using the `var` keyword:

```
var list = ["Legos", "Dungeons and Dragons", "Gameboy", "Monopoly", "Rubix
Cube"]
```

After doing so, we should be able to run this code without any problem:

```
list[4] = "Crayons"
```

If we decide to print the entire array, we will see the following print to console:

```
["Legos", "Dungeons and Dragons", "Gameboy", "Monopoly", "Crayons"]
```

Note how `Rubix Cube` is no longer the value at index 4 (our last index); it has been changed to `Crayons`.

That's how we can mutate (or change) elements at certain indexes in our array. What if we want to add a new item to the array. How do we do that? We've just seen that trying to use subscript syntax with an index that doesn't exist in our array crashes our application, so we know we can't use that to add new items to our array.

In the last chapter, you learned how to create functions. Apple (having created Swift) has created hundreds, if not thousands, of functions that are available in all the different types (like `String`, `Int`, and array). You can consider yourself an instance of a person (person being the name of the type). Being an instance of a person, you can run, eat, sleep, study, and exercise (among other things). These things are considered functions (or methods) that are available to you. Your pet rock doesn't have these functions available to it. Why? This is because it's an instance of a rock and not an instance of a person. An instance of a rock doesn't have the same functions available to it that an instance of a person has.

All that being said, an array can do things that a `String` and `Int` can't do. No, arrays can't run or eat, but they can append (or add) new items to themselves. An array can do this by calling the `append(_:)` method available to it. This method can be called on an instance of an array (like the preceding list), using what is known as dot syntax. In dot syntax, you write the name of the method immediately after the instance name, separated by a period (`.`), without any space:

```
list.append("Play-Doh")
```

Just as if we were to tell a person to run, we are telling the list to append. However, we can't just tell it to append, we have to pass an argument to the append function so that it can add it to the list.

Our list array now looks like this:

```
["Legos", "Dungeons and Dragons", "Gameboy", "Monopoly", "Crayons", "Play-Doh"]
```

We have covered a lot of material important to understanding Swift and writing iOS apps here. Feel free to reread what you've read so far, as well as writing code in a playground file. Create your own arrays, add whatever items you want to them, and change values at certain indexes. Get used to the syntax of working on creating arrays, as well as appending new items. If you feel comfortable up to this point with how arrays work, that's awesome; keep up the great work!

Dictionary

After a long day of figuring out what you wanted to bring with you, you received the greatest gift of all. After first landing on the moon, humans began to create their own language in space, called *Moon Speak*. After many decades, there were enough words to create a dictionary, which was titled *Moon Speak*. You now have this dictionary!

Just like dictionaries on Earth, you open the book to find a certain word. After finding that word, next to it is its definition.

If we were to open up a regular dictionary and look for the word *coffee*, we would be met with its definition, as follows:

Coffee : A drink made from the roasted and ground bean-like seeds of a tropical shrub, served hot or iced.

Let's associate words with these two items here:

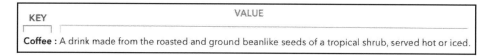

In order to retrieve this particular value here that represents the definition, we first need the key. The key here is the word coffee. If we hand you the key *Turtle*, you will use this key and the dictionary to retrieve the value, the value being the definition. If you plug the key *Turtle* into a dictionary, you should get the following value:

A slow-moving reptile, enclosed in a scaly or leathery domed shell into which it can retract its head and thick legs.

There's a type in Swift (just like `String`, `Int`, and array are types) that works just like a dictionary in real life. In fact, it's called a dictionary. A dictionary stores associations between keys of the same type and values of the same type in a collection with no defined ordering.

Hm, well that sounds like a real life dictionary, except for one part. What does it mean to not have defined ordering? One day, you might go through your dictionary and note that the first page has all words that begin with the letter *Z*. Every other time you open this dictionary, the pages will be different. So the next time you open the dictionary, you might note that the first page has all words that begin with the letter *B*. We will discuss this in detail later.

Let's create a `Dictionary` in Swift now:

```
var words = ["Coffee" : "A drink made from the roasted and ground beanlike
seeds of a tropical shrub, served hot or iced."]
```

That's it! It kind of looks a bit like creating an array, except for one big difference. Can you spot it? The colon (`:`) is the difference. When creating a Dictionary in Swift, you need to separate the key and the value by a colon and then enclose that in square brackets (like an array). We've created an instance of a dictionary where the keys are of the `String` type and the values are of the `String` type.

You describe the type of words by enclosing the type of the keys and the type of the values with a colon in between within square brackets, like so: `[String : String]`. words is a variable of the `[String : String]` type. It's a dictionary where the keys are of the `String` type and the values are of the `String` type. If we were was to hold *Alt* and select the `words` variable in playground, we would be met with the following screenshot, which confirms the type of our dictionary:

```
36 let words = ["Coffee" : "A drink made from the roasted
            seeds of a tropical shrub,
            "]

   Declaration   let words: [String : String]
   Declared In   Chapter7.playground
```

Let's create a new dictionary where the keys are of the `String` type and the values are of the `Int` type. This dictionary will be about the planets. The keys will represent the names of the planets and the values will represent the number of moons on each of those planets:

```
let planets = ["Earth" : 1, "Mars" : 2, "Jupiter" : 53]
```

Fun fact–Jupiter has the biggest moon in our solar system, named *Ganymede*.

When creating a dictionary that has multiple key-value pairs (like planets), we separate the various key-value pairs with commas. Don't forget, dictionaries are unordered in Swift, so there's no concept of indexes. `"Earth" : 1` is *not* considered to be at index 0; again, that's because they are not ordered.

This dictionary has three keys in it: `Earth`, `Mars`, and `Jupiter`. How, though, do we retrieve their values?

We can retrieve their values using the subscript syntax, which is similar to how we retrieve values from arrays (except without the index):

```
planets["Earth"]
```

The value we get back is 1. This is how we use the key (`Earth`) with our dictionary (`planets`) to retrieve the value (1) at that particular key (`Earth`).

If we want to store the value in a constant, we would do so like this:

```
let earthMoons = planets["Earth"]
```

We've created a constant named `earthMoons` and we are assigning it a value. The value being whatever is stored at the key `Earth` within the `planets` dictionary. Plugging this key `Earth` into the dictionary, we will get back the value stored for that particular key. The value returned here will be assigned to the `earthMoons` constant.

What if we want to create a new key-value pair within our dictionary. How can we do that? Similar to retrieving values at certain keys in a dictionary, we will use subscript syntax to add key-value pairs to a dictionary:

```
var favoriteColors = ["Neil" : "red", "Carl" : "blue"]
```

Here, we have a variable, called `favoriteColors`. We're assigning it a value that is a dictionary of the `[String : String]` type, where the keys represent names and the values represent their favorite colors.

If we want to add another key-value pair to this dictionary, we will do so as illustrated:

```
favoriteColors["Isaac"] = "green"
```

Now, our `favoriteColors` dictionary contains three key-value pairs, as we've just added a new one using subscript syntax. Creating a *new* key-value pair looks very similar to how we would retrieve a value from a dictionary; the difference being the (=) assignment operator, followed by the new value we want to associate with the key preceding the assignment operator:

```
print(favoriteColors)
// Prints "["Carl": "blue", "Isaac": "green", "Neil": "red"]"
```

What if we want to change a value for a certain key? Carl comes back to us to tell us that his favorite color is *white*.

Here's how we can change his favorite color to *white*:

```
favoriteColors["Carl"] = "white"
```

It's the exact same syntax that we use to create a new key-value pair. What's happening here is that *if* there already is a key-value pair within the dictionary that exists for the `Carl` key (which there is), then this will override it. This will change the value to `white` now, instead of `blue` for the `Carl` key.

Optionals

You might have noted something *odd* if you attempted to retrieve a value for a certain key from the preceding dictionaries and tried to print out the value to console. Let's do that now to see what it looks like.

Sticking to our `favoriteColors` dictionary, let's look to print out Carl's favorite color. First, we will store the value in a constant called `carlsFavColor`:

```
let carlsFavColor = favoriteColors["Carl"]
```

Let's use the print function to print out this constant to console:

```
print(carlsFavColor)
// prints "Optional("white")"
```

Shouldn't it be printing just the value `white`? What is this word `Optional` in front of the value `"white"` surrounded by parenthesis?

Before we step into that, let's do one more thing. What if I asked you to retrieve Jessica's favorite color from this `favoriteColors` dictionary? You might attempt something like this:

```
let jessFavColor = favoriteColors["Jessica"]
```

Well, wait a minute. `Jessica` doesn't exist as a key in our dictionary. So what happens? What is the value that is retrieved and stored in this `jessFavColor` constant?

Let's find out:

```
print(jessFavColor)
// prints "nil"
```

In retrieving a value from a dictionary, these values we get are represented as optionals. An optional value either contains a value or contains `nil` to indicate that a value is missing. We like to think of an optional value as a wrapped present:

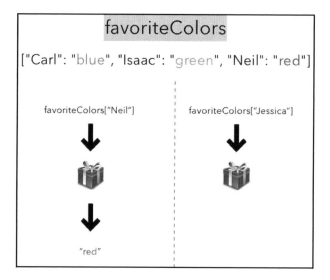

In our retrieval of a value from a dictionary, we will *always* get back a present (or an optional). In order for us to see what value we might have received from the dictionary, we need to open the present! This present is what's referred to as an optional. When we open it, it will either contain a value or it will be an empty box, where it doesn't contain any value (`nil`).

Okay, so optionals are like presents that need to be opened. Why is it like that? Why did Swift set it up this way? Well, if you *really* think about it, there might be scenarios in your code when you look to grab something from a dictionary where there is no such key (like our Jessica example).

A dictionary will *always* return an `Optional` when you're looking to grab a specific value with a key (like our preceding examples). In order to use the value at a certain key in a dictionary, we need to unwrap the optional, because if we don't, we saw what will happen when we attempted to print `carlsFavColor` earlier. It prints out the following output:

```
"Optional("white")"
```

The next chapter will further explain what a conditional is, but for now, we will show you the bare minimum to see how you unwrap the present (optional).

Think of a conditional statement as asking a question to someone, then getting a response. Based on that response, we perform a certain action. Imagine that you want to ask your sister whether or not her favorite color is blue. She can only answer by stating `true` or `false`. If she answers `true`, then we throw up our hands and say "*Hooray!*":

```
if true {
    "Hooray!"
}
```

We only enter those curly braces in the preceding code if our sister's response is `true`. That is what's referred to as an if-statement. If the condition (asking her if her favorite color is blue?) evaluates to `true` (meaning that she answered true), then we enter the following curly braces and scream out `Hooray!`. Note that, if she said `false`, we would not enter those curly braces and we would not be shouting out *Hooray!*.

We can use this logic to check weather a gift exists in our present! The correct term is looking to see if there's a value in our optional:

```
let carlsFavColor = favoriteColors["Carl"]
```

We know how to write this piece of code. Here, we've created a constant called `carlsFavColor` and we've assigned it a value; the value being whatever is stored at the `Carl` key within the `favoriteColors` dictionary. We just learned, though, that no matter what, a dictionary will always return an optional when you try to retrieve a value with a key.

All we have to do is throw in an `if` statement and some curly braces and we should be good to go! We'll leave our code the way it is and just add an if statement in front of the let keyword, as shown:

```
if let carlsFavColor = favoriteColors["Carl"]
```

Now we need to add one more thing, the curly braces:

```
if let carlsFavColor = favoriteColors["Carl"] {
    print("Hooray!")
    print(carlsFavColor)
}
// Prints "Hooray!"
// Prints "white"
```

The word used to describe this process using if-let is known as **optional binding.** `carlsFavColor` is now equal to the value `white`. It is not equal to `Optional("white")` as it was when we first attempted to retrieve the value using the `Carl` key in our preceding examples. The reason for this is that we have unwrapped our gift and stored whatever was in that gift in the `carlsFavColor` constant using optional binding.

In using optional binding, if we attempt to retrieve a value for a key that doesn't exist in our dictionary, we will not enter the curly braces and none of that code will be executed. It means that it opened up the gift to find no present (it is `nil`):

```
if let jessicaFavColor = favoriteColors["Jessica"] {
    print("Hooray!")
    print(jessicaFavColor)
}
// Nothing prints!
```

This is by no means an easy concept. We recommend that you open up Xcode (playground file), attempt to create your own dictionary and try to retrieve values from that dictionary with the keys of that dictionary using optional binding.

Summary

In this chapter, we introduced you to some of the most powerful types provided by the Swift language. Now that we know how to group various values, we can begin to think about how we can build the iOS applications that we have in mind. Before we get too ahead of ourselves, we need to talk about control flow. The next chapter will discuss working with collection types in detail. There are certain paths you will want to take in your code based upon certain conditions.

For example, if the light is green, then we can go. If the light is red, then we should stop. These are certain conditions that dictate how we move forward. How we handle this in code is discussed in detail in the next chapter.

8
Smarter Toy Bin

In any iOS application, there are certain conditions that need to be met before we do something. For example, if we're hungry, we should eat! If we're tired, we should go to sleep. Along with working with conditions like this, we will also take a closer look at working with collection types.

This chapter will introduce you to the following tools in Swift:

- For loops, which allow us to iterate over collections, sequences, and strings to be able to read all the values contained within them
- If-else statements to satisfy certain conditions, such as *if I'm hungry, then I should eat!*

Buttercup

After finally making it to the moon, without a day's rest, we were tasked with a job. All the other kids who were about to land on the moon had toy bins of their own. We were tasked to go through all these toy bins and throw away a particular flower that had a name we'd never heard of before. The name of this flower is Buttercup:

Being the Swift developer that we are, we've decided to write a program to handle this for us. For us (as humans) to go through each item one at a time from every single toy bin, it might take us forever to finish!

Getting right to it, we decided to create a function to handle this problem for us. This function will need to have one argument. When we look to call on this function, we will be giving it something; the something being an array of strings. That array of strings represents all the different items belonging to one person (their toy bin). In our implementation of this function, we will first create a new empty array (or new empty toy bin), and then go through each item from the array given to us. If we find that the item isn't the Buttercup flower, then we will add it to our new array. After we're done with this, we will return to the caller of this function, the new array containing all kinds of items excluding Buttercup flowers. Here is that code:

```swift
func removeBadItems(list: [String]) -> [String] {
    var newList: [String] = []
    for item in list {
        if item == "Buttercup" {
            print("Sorry, you're not allowed to bring that here to the
Moon.")
        } else {
            newList.append(item)
        }
    }
    return newList
}
```

All related source code for this chapter can be found here: `https://githu b.com/swift-book-projects/swift-3-programming-for-kids/tree/ma ster/Chapter-8`

This is the answer, but why are we showing it to you so early? We will be stepping through every bit of this function to ensure that you understand every single part. Give it a try though. Go through the preceding code line by line and see if you can understand what's going on:

What's currently highlighted in the preceding screenshot is what we will be going over first:

```
var newList: [String] = []
```

We've created a new variable, named `newList`, of the `[String]` type. We've also assigned it a value (using the assignment operator =); the value being an empty array denoted by two square brackets, `[]`.

This represents the new array (or list) we made that will not contain the Buttercup value. We will ensure that it will contain all the other types of items as we progress through our function's implementation:

```
func removeBadItems(list: [String]) -> [String] {
    var newList: [String] = []
    for item in list {
        if item == "Buttercup" {
            print("Sorry, you're not allowed to bring that
                  here to the Moon.")
        } else {
            newList.append(item)
        }
    }
    return newList
}
```

In the next section, we will discuss the for-in loop.

Learning the for-in loop

This is an interesting piece of code; it's referred to as a for-in loop. It loops through every single item in our array. Here is an example of the same:

```
for item in list {

}
```

In the preceding example, item is a constant whose value is automatically set at the beginning of each iteration of the loop. It means that item changes to reflect a new value after each iteration of the loop. It also means that item can be used only within the scope of the for-in loop:

```
1 let list = [1, 2, 3]
2
3 for item in list {
4
5     // Within the scope of the for-in loop
6
7 }
8
9 // NOT within the scope
```

Let's create an array, called `list`, and assign it a value; the value being an array of integers (`[Int]`). If we were to loop over this array using the for-in syntax we just learned, we would need to give a name to the constant whose value will change through each iteration of the for-in loop. The name we give it should make sense, which means that it should pertain, in some way, to the items in the array. Here, we've decided to use the word `item`, but it might have made more sense to use the word number, as we know our list array contains only `Int` values. The name you provide for this constant should not be plural.

The following is a diagram representing how a for-in loop works. It begins by assigning the first value in our array to the constant called `item`. Our for-in loop will be executed three times, beginning with the first element in the array and ending with the last. The first time through the for-in loop, `item` is assigned the value 1. The second time through the for-in loop, `item` is assigned the value 2. The third (and last) time through the for-in loop, `item` is assigned the value 3:

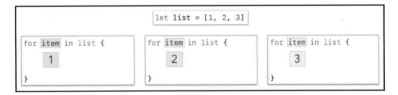

Let's add a print statement to a for-in loop to see this in action:

```
let list = [1, 2, 3]
for item in list {
    print(item)
}
// Prints "1"
// Prints "2"
// Prints "3"
```

What if we did something like this. What do you think would print to the console?

```
let names = ["Jessica", "Beth", "Rebecca"]
for name in names {
    print("My best friend is \(name).")
}
```

The first time through this for-in loop, `name` (being a constant) is assigned the value Jessica because Jessica is the first item in the `names` array. Our first time through the for-in loop, we call on the `print` function, which will print `"My best friend is \(name).",` to the console. Using string interpolation, `name` will be replaced by its value when this `String` is created. So, the first time through, `name` is equal to Jessica, which will print `My best friend is Jessica`. The second time through the for-in loop, `name` is assigned the value `Beth`. Similar to the first time through, we call on the `print` statement again and when the `String` is generated, `name` has a different value (it's now `Beth`), so the `String` generated is `My best friend is Beth`. The third and final time through, `name` has the value `Rebecca`. The `String` generated is `My best friend is Rebecca`:

This is really powerful stuff! This for-in loop can do a lot of the work for us when we try to solve our original problem of excluding all items named Buttercup.

Instead of just printing out the `name` constant, we can do other things with it. It's no different than any other `String` constant or variable we made in previous chapters. However, considering that it's a constant, we can't mutate it (change its value to something different). Holding down the *option* key and then selecting `name` in the for-in loop, we can see that it is actually a constant (declared with the `let` keyword):

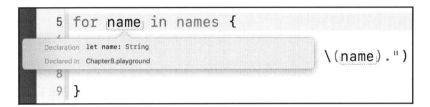

So, besides printing the name constant, what else can we do with it? Well, we can check to see that it isn't equal to the word Buttercup. How do we do that in code?

Conditionals

Before putting pen to paper (or in our case, finger tip to keyboard), we should think through the exact problem we're trying to solve here. We should first check to see whether we can explain the problem we're trying to solve in English, and after doing so, we should try to produce it in code.

If `name` *is equal* to the word Buttercup, then ignore it! If it's equal to anything else (besides Buttercup), then we should keep it.

How do we handle the *is equal* part in code? We do so using the == operator in Swift, which is two equal signs next to each other. This tells the compiler that it will take the thing (or value) to the left-hand side of this == operator, compare it to the thing (or value) to the right-hand side of the == operator and return `true` if they *equal* or return `false` if they are *not equal*. The following code uses the == operator:

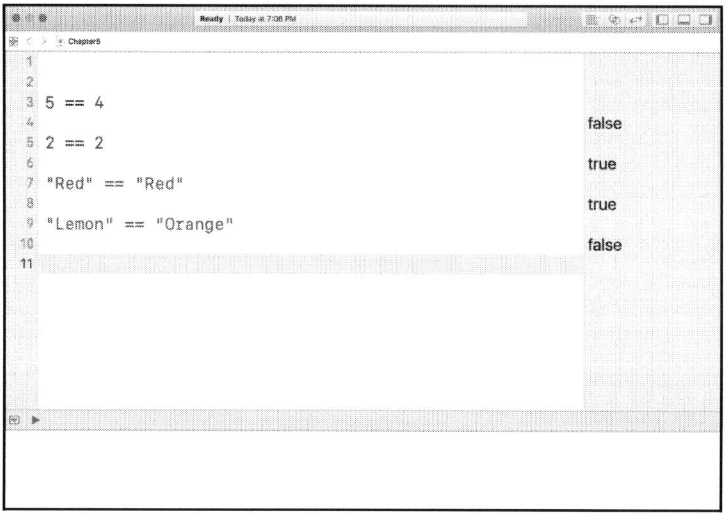

If using this operator returns either the value `true` or the value `false`, we can use this to our advantage. Now we need to satisfy the if portion of our preceding sentence.

If `true`, do one thing, if `false`, do another thing.

We satisfy the if portion of our sentence here using the if-statement, as shown:

```
if 5 == 4 {
    print ("I'm eating an apple.")
}
```

We could have also wrapped 5 == 4 within parentheses like so:

```
if (5 == 4) {
    print ("I'm eating an apple.")
}
```

Both if-statements would evaluate to the same value, there is no difference between the two. Parentheses are optional but the braces are required.

We have a question for you. Do you think `I'm eating an apple.` will print to the console? If the answer to that question is no, then why?

Only if what we're checking here evaluates to `true` do we enter into the braces which contain the `print` statement. You can refer to being in a set of braces as being in a specific scope. So, when we state that we're within the scope of something, it usually pertains to being in a set of braces `{}`.

We will only execute the `print` statement here if what we're checking evaluates to `true`. As 5 does not equal 4 (the if-statement evaluates to `false`), we *do not* enter the following braces and we do not print out `I'm eating an apple.` to console.

What if we changed our if-statement to read something like this:

```
if 4 == 4 {
    print("I'm eating an apple.")
}
```

If 4 is equal to 4 (which it is), that statement evaluates to `true`. Preceding this piece of code (4 `==` 4) is the `if` keyword. That is how you create an if-statement. If 4 `==` 4 evaluates to `true` (which it does), then we enter the following set of braces. Included in those braces is the `print` statement printing `I'm eating an apple.`, which will actually run and print to console.

If 5 `==` 4 does not equal `true`, in that it evaluates to `false` (which it does), can we handle that situation? We can. This is considered an else statement, which we will explain shortly.

Let's paint a different scenario. Let's say that your favorite color is Blue and our favorite color is Red:

```
let yourFavoriteColor = "Blue"
let ourFavoriteColor = "Red"
```

If your favorite color is equal to our favorite color, then we will print `We both love the color red!` If we don't share the same favorite color, then we will print `Ugh. Just like everything else, we differ on favorite colors.`

We handle this `else` case as illustrated in this code:

```
if yourFavoriteColor == mourFavoriteColor {
    print("We all love the color red!")
} else {
    print("Ugh. Just like everything else, we differ on favorite colors")
}
```

Well, this looks kind of funny now. The `else` case here follows the `if` case. As soon as the if-statement's braces end, we've created an else-statement. It's created by writing the `else` keyword followed by a set of braces. We only enter the else-statement's braces if the if-statement preceding it evaluates to `false`.

This allows us to handle both `true` and `false` values when working with questions like we mentioned earlier.

Running through our preceding code, the following output will print to the console:

```
// Prints "Ugh. Just like everything else, we differ on favorite colors."
```

Let us now move on to for-loops and if-statements.

Learning for-loops and if-statements

Let's create another scenario. We have an array, `stuff`, which includes four `String` values representing different things someone might take with them to the moon. `stuff` is an array of `String` values, which you denote by being of type `[String]`. The following line of code is our creation of this `Array`:

```
let stuff = ["Coloring Book", "Marvel Comic", "Buttercup", "Moby Dick"]
```

We want to loop through each `String` value in this array and check to see whether or not any of the values are equal to `Buttercup`.

We know how to do this now, so let's do it. The following line of code is us first creating our for-in loop:

```
for thing in stuff {
    print(thing)
}
// Prints "Coloring Book"
// Prints "Marvel Comic"
// Prints "Buttercup"
// Prints "Moby Dick"
```

We don't want to just print the various items in this array; we want to inspect them and see whether or not any of the items are equal to Buttercup. The following code implements exactly this:

```
for thing in stuff {
    if thing == "Buttercup" {
        print("Ah hah! You are not allowed to take this \(thing) any
further.")
    } else {
        print("\(thing) is allowed. ")
    }
}

// Prints "Coloring Book is allowed."
// Prints "Marvel Comic is allowed."
// Prints "Ah hah! You are not allowed to take this Buttercup any further."
// Prints "Moby Dick is allowed."
```

You can get a good sense of what's happening here by reading just the `print` statements. We're looping over every single item one at a time. The value of `thing` changes through each iteration of the for-in loop. It begins by having the value `Coloring Book`, as `Coloring Book` is the first element in the array `stuff`, and ends with having the value `Moby Dick`, which is the last element in the array `stuff`.

Within the scope of the for-in loop, we've created an if-else statement. If `thing` (at its current value at the time) is equal to the `String` value `Buttercup`, then print out the statement `Ah hah! You are not allowed to take this \(thing) any further.`, `thing` being replaced with its current value at the time using string interpolation. We will only enter the else-statement here if our if-statement evaluates to `false` (`thing` not being equal to `Buttercup`). If we enter the else-statement, we will print `\(thing) is allowed.`, `thing` being replaced with its current value at the time.

One last thing to talk about before we go back to solving our original problem. Just like an instance of a car can perform certain methods such as, drive, steer, park, and get gas. Similarly, an array is a type in Swift. And, just like cars, Arrays have certain methods they can perform.

Append method

One of these methods, `append(_:)`, allows us to add new elements (or items) to an array.

Let's create an array called `animals`, with the following value:

```
var animals = ["Cat", "Dog", "Bird"]
```

`append(_:)` is a method only available to instances of an array, just like *drive* is a method only available to instances of car (the cars you see driving around on highways are considered instances of car, each being its own instance). This `append(_:)` method is called on our instance (our instance here being `animals`). We do this by typing out the name of our array instance (which is `animals`) and then typing a period. This period denotes that we will call a method or read one of its properties. After this period, you begin to type out the word `append`, which should then be autocompleted for you if you press the *return* key. Just like any other function you call on, you will be met with two parentheses, letting you know that this function requires that you pass it one argument. So, in our example here, we will pass this function the value "`Lion`" like so:

```
animals.append("Lion")
```

Now our `animals` array contains four different values; it now includes "`Lion`" in addition to the other three which you can see here:

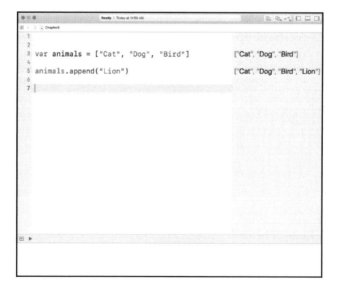

We will cover this subject of methods being called on instances in-depth in the coming chapters.

Find the buttercup

To test out our function, we're first creating an array called `stuff`. In a playground file, click on the square box in the right pane and it will display the contents of the array (below the variable). The **0**, **1**, **2**, and **3** numbers represent the index associated with the value at that index. As you've learned, arrays are indexed. So, at index `0` you should find the value **Coloring Book**:

```
1 let stuff = ["Coloring Book", "Marvel Comic", "Buttercup", "Moby Dick"]

   0 "Coloring Book"
   1 "Marvel Comic"
   2 "Buttercup"
   3 "Moby Dick"

2
3 func removeBadItems(list: [String]) -> [String] {
4     var newList: [String] = []
5     for item in list {
6         if item == "Buttercup" {
7             print("Sorry, you're not allowed to bring that here to the Moon.")
8         } else {
9             newList.append(item)
10        }
11    }
12    return newList
13 }
14
15 let validStuff = removeBadItems(list: stuff)

   0 "Coloring Book"
   1 "Marvel Comic"
   2 "Moby Dick"

Sorry, you're not allowed to bring that here to the Moon.
```

From what you've learned in this chapter, you should go through this function line by line to discern what it is that's actually happening and at what time. Give it your best shot! Look back at all the examples given in this chapter to help you. Don't rush through it either; it's important that you feel comfortable with these concepts. It's all about building more complexity on top of the basics, and if your core knowledge of Swift is strong, then it will make your further studies that much easier.

As you can see, `validStuff` is an array that contains all the same items that `stuff` has, except one thing–it doesn't contain Buttercup. This is exactly what we wanted to do. `removeBadItems(list:)` is a function that we made; it takes in one argument that we've labeled as `list`. Whomever calls on this function must give it an array of strings and this function will return an array of strings.

We will use this `removeBadItems(list:)` function by calling on it, passing it the value `stuff` as its only argument and then assigning the return value to a new constant called `validStuff`. This is what's happening in the preceding screenshot. The `stuff` array is an array of `String`, so we pass that along to our function call. After doing this, the function executes (because we called on it). It takes in an array of `String` (in this case, it takes in an array called `stuff` because that is what we passed to it in our example). In our implementation of this function, `list` is equal to `stuff`. Anywhere we type out the word `list` within the scope of this function, we're referring to the array that was passed into this method when someone called on it.

After the function completes all of its tasks within the for-in loop, we move on to the following line of code:

```
return newList
```

This is the last thing that executes within this function. First, it will have to finish the for-in loop. As soon as it loops through every item in the array, it will exit the scope of the for-in loop. We finally enter *line #13* (from within the playground file), which is this `return` statement. We are returning the new array (`newList`) we assembled within the for-in loop.

After being on the moon for one day, having solved this problem, and getting a chance to walk around to see the stars, we can honestly say that we've had the best day ever.

Summary

This chapter went in-depth in to how we can use for-in loops to solve certain problems in our code. Along with for-in loops, we were shown how to use if-else statements, which help us write code to satisfy certain conditions. These are two very powerful tools in Swift.

We now have a pretty clear understanding as to what a type in Swift is. We've seen types, such as `String`, `Int`, `Array`, and `Dictionary`, but what if we want to make our own custom type? We will be going through how to create our own custom types in the next chapter.

For example, if we want a type in our code to represent a Person, we will create our own Person type. An instance of this type would have a name and an address, along with a favorite ice cream flavor! It can also walk, run, and sleep. It sounds like we can solve this problem with variables and functions. This is what we will be covering in the next chapter.

9
Making Some Friends

The last couple of chapters have introduced a lot of central concepts in the world of programming and we're getting really close to being able to start writing some real programs for our iPhone. One important piece of the puzzle is a strategy to divide the different responsibilities of our code and model the things we are trying to solve with our program.

Object-Oriented Programming (OOP) is a strategy to design our programs and is supported by the Swift language and widely used among Swift developers. Designing our code base using an object-oriented approach makes it easier for us to map our human understanding of a real-world problem into our code. It also makes it easier for us to reason about our code, which is something we care a lot about when we program. The easier it is to reason about our code, the easier it is for us to remember what our intentions were when we wrote the code, and the easier it is for somebody else to help us maintain our code.

The main focus of this chapter is to:

- Give the reader a short introduction to the OOP paradigm
- Help the reader to visualize and remember the OOP paradigm using a person metaphor
- Give concrete examples of objects, instance properties, and instance methods

OOP

Steve Jobs, the former CEO of Apple and probably the person who people most often associate with Apple, was asked the question about what OOP is in an interview (http://www.rollingstone.com/culture/news/steve-jobs-in-1994-the-rolling-stone-interview-20110117#ixzz3CSNRGuIf) with the Rolling Stone magazine in 1994. Here is how he started explaining what OOP is:

> *Objects are like people. They're living, breathing things that have knowledge inside them about how to do things and have memory inside them so they can remember things. And rather than interacting with them at a very low level, you interact with them at a very high level of abstraction, like we're doing right here.*

Note how he suggests that we visualize objects as being people. This is similar to how we suggested one could visualize what a function is in Chapter 6, *Making Pizza*. He continues his explanation by giving an example:

> *Here's an example: If I'm your laundry object, you can give me your dirty clothes and send me a message that says, "Can you get my clothes laundered, please." I happen to know where the best laundry place in San Francisco is. I speak English, and I have dollars in my pockets. So, I go out and hail a taxicab and tell the driver to take me to this place in San Francisco. I go get your clothes laundered, I jump back in the cab, and I get back here. I give you your clean clothes and say, "Here are your clean clothes."*

Do you remember the characteristics of a function that we covered in Chapter 6, *Making Pizza*? Here they are:

- It can receive some input
- It can be pure
- It can return something

Steve Jobs's example of the laundry object seems to conform to these characteristics in the following senses:

- It received some input in the form of dirty clothes.
- It is self-contained in the sense that the person who asked the laundry object to launder their clothes does not know anything about how the task is being solved. All that logic about knowing where to go and how to launder the clothes is encapsulated or contained inside the laundry object.
- It returns something because the laundry object promises to return your clothes after they have been laundered.

In fact, as you will see later in the chapter, objects can expose functionality in terms of functions. Steve Jobs continues by saying the following words:

> *You have no idea how I did that. You have no knowledge of the laundry place. Maybe you speak French, and you can't even hail a taxi. You can't pay for one, you don't have dollars in your pocket. Yet I knew how to do all that and you didn't have to know any of it. All that complexity was hidden inside me, and we were able to interact at a very high level of abstraction. That's what objects are. They encapsulate complexity, and the interfaces to that complexity are high level.*

Interacting on a high level is central to OOP. Instead of relying on specific details, objects tend to communicate on an abstract level. In the example with the laundry object, all you needed to know in order to get your clothes laundered was that you should ask the laundry object to do it and give your clothes as an input. How the clothes are being laundered is none of your concern, as the laundry object promises to handle this task. On the other end, the laundry object does not need to know all the specific details. The laundry object does not care about where you bought your clothes from, how much they cost, or in what sizes they are. All it needs to know is that they are clothes and maybe it would need to know the wash care symbols in order to know how to launder them.

Modeling real-world objects

To get a better understanding of how we can model objects in OOP, let's try to go through a couple of examples from the real world. As you will see, there are a lot of similarities when we try to model real-world objects and objects in our programs.

Modeling a mug

Using our knowledge about what OOP is, let's look at a more concrete example. Let's take a look at the object in the following photograph:

Using our real-world knowledge combined with common sense, what could be some characteristics of this mug? Instead of considering the actual values or the specifics of the mug, let's try to come up with a set of properties this mug has. We could say that the mug has a color which is the color of the ceramic, which in this case is white. We could also say something about the print on the mug. Perhaps we could generalize this into being an image or print that a mug can have. Maybe we could also model the material of the mug, which in general could be glass, ceramic, or maybe something else. Lastly, we could say something about the size of the mug. We could have different categories of sizes of mugs, for example: small, medium, and big. To summarize, some of the characteristics of this mug could be as follows:

- Color
- Image
- Material
- Size

As you might have noted, these properties do not say a lot about this specific mug, but say more about mugs in general. This is central to OOP, where we tend to try and model abstract or generic things, as opposed to concrete things. If we want to model this mug using its specific properties, one can come up with the following values:

- White
- Postcard from Cuba
- Ceramic
- Medium

However, this is not very flexible when we want to deal with multiple mugs with different properties. Also, using abstractions makes it easier to deal with objects that are modeling the same thing. For example, let's say we want to model our mug using specific properties. One might explain the specifics of the mug using a foreign language, such as Japanese, using materials that are not common, or sizes measured in centimeters instead of inches. All these specific details complicate things when we want to communicate with objects. Instead, we try to rely on abstractions to simplify how we communicate using objects.

In this example, the model of our mug is called a **class**, which is a representation of a mug on an abstract level. The characteristics of our mug are called **properties**. When we instantiate our class it is referred to as an **object**, hence the name OOP. Using classes or specifications on an abstract level makes it possible for us to instantiate objects that share properties, but the values might be different. One mug might be blue and made of glass and the other one might be green and made of ceramic. In Chapter 5, *Factories*, we saw how to instantiate various types, including a String type:

```
let myString = "This is my string"
```

This is very similar to our example with the mug. Instead of modeling a string as something concrete, we model a string as something abstract that can hold a value (in this case, the characters that form our sentence). Using the representation of our mug, we should be able to instantiate a mug with the values we need for a specific object.

Modeling a person

A person could be modeled as an object in the same way we modeled a mug. A person has a lot of different properties, which could also be modeled in an abstract way. Take a look at the person in the following photograph:

The abstract properties for a person could be as listed:

- Name
- Age
- Hair color
- Skin color
- Height
- Weight

These are all properties that are not unique to the person in the picture, but are shared by all persons. Although properties tell us a lot about an object, or in this case, a person, they do not tell us a lot about how objects communicate or perform tasks. How would you know that our model of a person is able to jump, dance, or greet another person object? None of this information is exposed in properties.

While we can think of properties as being the characteristics of an object (that might change over time), **methods**, on the other hand, tell us what that object is capable of doing. Instead of just holding a plain value for a property, methods are able to perform some encapsulated work. Let's revisit a paragraph from Chapter 6, *Making Pizza*:

To help visualize what a function is, we can think of it as being a person performing a specific task–a person working at the pizza joint who writes down the order when we call them; a person who finds the next order in the queue; a person who takes the order and makes the pizza; and finally, a person who grabs the pizza and delivers it to you. We can think of the function being a person responsible for one specific task that we can ask the person to perform.

That sounds a lot like how we just described methods. In fact, they are more or less the same thing. The only difference is that when a function becomes part of an object, we call it a method. This means that if an object exposes a function it can perform, we call it a method. If somewhere in our program we have defined a function, we will be able to call that function without having to instantiate an object. Now that we know that methods are functions tied to an object, what could be examples of methods tied to a person? What about jumping?

Let's revisit the three characteristics of a function from Chapter 6, *Making Pizza*:

- It can receive some input
- It can be pure
- It can return something

What could be the input for a person in order to be able to perform a jump? Maybe some sort of an indication of how high the person should jump. It could also be an indication of whether the person should jump using both feet or just one. All these could be reasonable input to a person in the real world, as well as in our code when we try to model a person as an object. The input could also be another person, in order for them to jump at the same time.

We also described functions as being self-contained in the sense that they are able to perform a task without involving anything or anybody else. In the example of a person performing a jump, it is reasonable to say that this task is self-contained.

Lastly, a function can return something. Does it make sense for a person to return something after performing a jump? Maybe not, but it might make sense to know when a person is done jumping. How else would you know when the person is ready to jump again? It does not make a lot of sense to keep telling a person to jump if they never get to finish their first jump before being ordered to do a second jump.

Our first class

Go ahead and create a new Xcode playground and delete the autogenerated content. Let's continue with our example of modeling a person by adding the following to our playground:

```
class Person {

}
```

 All related source code for this chapter can be found here: `https://githu b.com/swift-book-projects/swift-3-programming-for-kids/tree/ma ster/Chapter-9`

Let's take a look at the simple code we just wrote. The `class` keyword is how we define a class in Swift. Remember that a class is our abstract representation of something we are trying to model and the object is the instance of our class. Next, `Person` is the name of our class, and is also called our type. In Swift, we capitalize the names of our classes. This is similar to other types we have seen so far, such as `String` and `Int`; the difference being that this is a type that we define ourselves.

If we want to instantiate our new class that does not hold any functionality, we will do it by writing the following code:

```
let bob = Person()
```

This means that we now have an object of the `Person` class, which we can now reference using the `bob` constant.

Instance properties

A class without properties or methods is not much fun, so let's look at how we can add some properties to our new class. We already discussed what properties could be associated with a person, so let's go ahead and add some of these to our class:

```
class Person {
    var name: String
    var age: Int
    var hairColor: String
}
```

At this point, Xcode will throw a couple of errors, but let's not worry about that for now. We added the following three properties to our class:

- `name` is the name of our person. The type is a `String`.
- `age` is the age of our person. The type is `Int`, which means that we only care about natural numbers.
- `hairColor` is the hair color of our person. The type is `String`.

Xcode is throwing errors because we defined our types as not being optional. If you recall from `Chapter 7`, *Toy Bin*, optional allows a property to not have a value (or to be `nil`). In our class, we are not allowing this for our properties to simplify the example. It might be that a person has not been baptized and, because of that, is without a name. It might also be that a person is bald, which means that it is hard to determine the person's hair color. However, let's simplify our person class by always requiring our properties to have values.

To fix these errors, we can add an initializer, making it possible to initialize an instance of our class with some given values:

```
init(name: String, age: Int, hairColor: String) {
    self.name = name
    self.age = age
    self.hairColor = hairColor
}
```

This initializer is essentially a special kind of method that allows us to create an instance of our person. Note how the parameters match the properties we have added to our class. Inside the method body, we simply set each value of the method to the properties of our class. When we are inside a method and in the event of overlapping property names, we can distinguish the parameters from the class properties by referring to class properties using the `self` keyword. At this point, your playground should look like this:

Note how we're still seeing an error in Xcode:

Xcode is letting us know that in order to make an instance of our person class, we need to provide a name. This is because of the special `init` method we just added, which will be used automatically when we try to make an instance of our class. However, even though we add a name to our method call, it will complain afterwards about a missing argument for the age. In order to satisfy Xcode, we need to provide values for all three parameters in our `init` method:

```
let bob = Person(name: "Bob", age: 13, hairColor: "black")
```

In order to retrieve the values of our instance, we can use the dot notation and then reference the property we want to access; for example, `bob.name` to get the name of the person. To verify that we actually created a correct instance of a person, we can add this `print` statement to our program:

```
print("My name is \(bob.name), I am \(bob.age) years old and my hair color
is \(bob.hairColor).")
```

If you take a look at the console, the output should now correctly output the values we set to instantiate `bob`:

The console should be saying `My name is Bob, I am 13 years and my hair color is black.`, which makes sense because we created our instance with the `Bob`, `13`, and `black` values.

Instance methods

At this point, we have our own class that is trying to model a person. We have added properties to our person in order for us to easily represent a person. The next thing we can look at is how to add tasks that can be performed by our person class. In other words, adding instance methods. We discussed earlier that it made sense for a person to be able to jump. Let's try and add this behavior to our class. The simplest approach to this behavior is to add a method that does not take any input and does not return anything. All it does is to simulate that it is jumping by printing that to the console:

```
func jump() {
    print("\(self.name) is jumping")
}
```

This way of creating a function should be familiar, as this is how we did it back in Chapter 6, *Making Pizza*. The only difference is that we're now referencing the instance using the self keyword; in this case, we're saying the name of the instance that has been created is jumping. Remember that a class is like a blueprint and an instance of a class is an object. Instance methods are tied to the object which makes it possible for us to reference the name of the person that is jumping. Adding this method to our class looks like this:

```
class Person {
    var name: String
    var age: Int
    var hairColor: String

    init(name: String, age: Int, hairColor: String) {
        self.name = name
        self.age = age
        self.hairColor = hairColor
    }

    func jump() {
        print("\(self.name) is jumping")
    }
}
```

Let's try and call our newly added method:

```
jump()
```

Wait a second, now Xcode starts reporting an error saying that it cannot find our new function:

```
19 jump()|                                    Use of unresolved identifier 'jump'
```

How can that be? This is the difference between a function and an instance method. Remember that we placed our new `jump` method inside our class. This means that we are only able to call it on an instance of `Person`. If we move the method outside the class, then it will be a function and we can call it just by typing `jump()`. So, in order to call this function, we can use our `bob` instance to make him jump:

```
bob.jump()
```

If we take a look at Xcode, it should show in the console that `Bob is jumping`:

```
 1 class Person {
 2     var name: String
 3     var age: Int
 4     var hairColor: String
 5
 6     init(name: String, age: Int, hairColor: String) {
 7         self.name = name
 8         self.age = age
 9         self.hairColor = hairColor
10     }
11
12     func jump() {
13         print("\(self.name) is jumping")          "Bob is jumping\n"
14     }
15 }
16
17 let bob = Person(name: "Bob", age: 13, hairColor:      Person
      "black")
18 bob.jump()|                                            Person
19
```

```
Bob is jumping
```

How cool is that? We are now able to instantiate our `Person` class with a set of values and simulate that our person performs a task.

Making objects interact with each other

Let's continue to develop our person class by adding more methods. We can, for example, make our class able to greet, as shown:

```
func greet() {
    print("\(self.name) is greeting")
}
```

This method is very similar to our `jump` method, the only difference being the name of the method and the simulation that goes on inside the method body.

Usually when we greet, we do it to greet other people, why should our `Person` class be any different? We can add a parameter to our `greet` method that takes in an instance of another person. This is similar to saying that we want our person instance to greet the person we give as input. The function will then look like this:

```
func greet(person: Person) {
    print("\(self.name) greets \(person.name)")
}
```

Note how the first name is being printed using the `self` keyword, which means that this refers to the instance that is being asked to perform this task. The input is of the `Person` type and can be referenced using the `person` label. Therefore, in order to print out the name of the person we asked our instance to greet, we use `person.name`. The last part is very similar to how we used parameter values in Chapter 6, *Making Pizza*.

In order to use our new method, we need two instances of a person:

```
let bob = Person(name: "Bob", age: 13, hairColor: "black")
let alice = Person(name: "Alice", age: 12, hairColor: "blonde")
```

We are reusing our code from earlier to instantiate Bob, but we have added another line of code that takes care of instantiating Alice. Now, in order to make Bob greet Alice, we need to call the instance method on Bob, passing Alice as input:

```
bob.greet(person: alice)
```

If we take a look at the console, it should say `Bob greets Alice`:

How cool is that? We just made two instances of a person communicate using the knowledge we acquired on OOP. In particular, note how the objects are communicating using the abstract `Person` type.

Adding more classes to the mix

Let's extend our program by introducing another class. We could add a `Dog` class to represent a dog that our persons are able to interact with. It could look something like this:

```
class Dog {
    var name: String
    var age: Int
    var breed: String

    init(name: String, age: Int, breed: String) {
        self.name = name
        self.age = age
        self.breed = breed
    }
}
```

Very similar to our `Person` class, our new `Dog` class has the following properties:

- `name` is the name of the dog
- `age` is the age of the dog
- `breed` is the breed of the dog

To instantiate a dog, we follow a similar pattern as with our `Person` class by writing the following code:

```
let max = Dog(name: "Max", age: 5, breed: "golden retriever")
```

We can combine our objects by allowing a person to have a pet. Now that we have our `Dog` type, we can use that to update our `Person` class by adding one more property:

```
var pet: Dog?
```

In this case, we are making it optional for a person to have a pet; this allows us to use the same initializer and avoid having to update how we created Bob and Alice.

 In Swift, a question mark (?) after the value of an object is used to mark the value as optional.

Let's add another instance method to our `Person` class that uses this new `pet` property. We can, for example, make it possible for a person to play fetch with their pet:

```
func playFetch() {
    if let unwrappedPet = self.pet {
        print("\(self.name) is playing fetch with \(unwrappedPet.name)")
    } else {
        print("\(self.name) cannot play fetch as he haven't got any pet")
    }
}
```

In the method body of `playFetch`, we are first unwrapping the optional `pet` property of the `Person` instance. As this property is optional, we do not know whether or not it has been set. If the person has a pet, we simulate that they play fetch together. If they do not have a pet, we print a small message saying that the person cannot play fetch, because the person does not have a pet. Note how `playFetch` is not taking in any pet as a parameter. This is intentional, as the purpose of this function is to encapsulate the task of playing fetch with the pet a person owns (if any).

This means that we rely on the instance property of pet. At this point, your playground should look something like this:

```
1  class Person {
2      var name: String
3      var age: Int
4      var hairColor: String
5      var pet: Dog?
6
7      init(name: String, age: Int, hairColor: String) {
8          self.name = name
9          self.age = age
10         self.hairColor = hairColor
11     }
12
13     func jump() {
14         print("\(self.name) is jumping")
15     }
16
17     func greet(person: Person) {
18         print("\(self.name) greets \(person.name)")          "Bob greets Alice\...
19     }
20
21     func playFetch() {
22         if let unwrappedPet = self.pet {
23             print("\(self.name) is playing fetch with \
                   (unwrappedPet.name)")
24         } else {
25             print("\(self.name) cannot play fetch as he
                   haven't got any pet")
26         }
27     }
28 }
29
```

The lower portion of the playground would look like this:

```
30  class Dog {
31      var name: String
32      var age: Int
33      var breed: String
34
35      init(name: String, age: Int, breed: String) {
36          self.name = name
37          self.age = age
38          self.breed = breed
39      }
40  }
41
42  let bob = Person(name: "Bob", age: 13, hairColor:        Person
        "black")
43  let alice = Person(name: "Alice", age: 12, hairColor:    Person
        "blonde")
44  bob.greet(person: alice)                                 Person
45
46  let max = Dog(name: "Max", age: 5, breed: "golden        Dog
        retriever")

Bob greets Alice
```

If we want to check whether our `playFetch` method works as intended, we can try to ask Bob to play fetch:

```
bob.playFetch()
```

If you look at the console, it should say `Bob cannot play fetch as he haven't got any pet`, which makes sense because we haven't set which pet Bob has. Let's try and make Max Bob's pet:

```
bob.pet = max
```

Now, if we try and make Bob play fetch again, the result should be different:

```
1  class Person {
2      var name: String
3      var age: Int
4      var hairColor: String
5      var pet: Dog?
6
7      init(name: String, age: Int, hairColor: String) {
8          self.name = name
9          self.age = age
10         self.hairColor = hairColor
11     }
12
13     func jump() {
14         print("\(self.name) is jumping")
15     }
16
17     func greet(person: Person) {
18         print("\(self.name) greets \(person.name)")       "Bob greets A...
19     }
20
21     func playFetch() {
22         if let unwrappedPet = self.pet {
23             print("\(self.name) is playing fetch with \    "Bob is playin...
                   (unwrappedPet.name)")
24         } else {
25             print("\(self.name) cannot play fetch as he
                   haven't got any pet")
26         }
27     }
28 }
```

The result would be as shown below:

```
class Dog {
    var name: String
    var age: Int
    var breed: String

    init(name: String, age: Int, breed: String) {
        self.name = name
        self.age = age
        self.breed = breed
    }
}

let bob = Person(name: "Bob", age: 13, hairColor: "black")      Person
let alice = Person(name: "Alice", age: 12, hairColor:           Person
    "blonde")
bob.greet(person: alice)                                        Person

let max = Dog(name: "Max", age: 5, breed: "golden              Dog
    retriever")
bob.pet = max                                                   Person
bob.playFetch()                                                 Person
```

```
Bob greets Alice
Bob is playing fetch with Max
```

Feel free to try and create other instances of our `Person` class and make them perform tasks and interact with each other.

Summary

In this chapter, the popular programming paradigm OOP was introduced. Without going into too many technical details, we looked at the characteristics of this pattern based on how Steve Jobs once explained what it is. We looked at several examples of how to apply this on a metaphorical level.

The second part of this chapter dived into how we can create classes in Swift. More precisely, we looked at the following things:

- How to create classes
- How to add instance properties to classes
- How to add instance methods to classes
- How objects can communicate with each other

The chapter ended with a program that combined a lot of what has been covered in this chapter, as well as in earlier chapters.

In the next chapter, we will continue building on what we have learned so far. We will be doing this by creating a small PokÃ©mon game where we are able to create instances of PokÃ©mons that are able to fight each other.

10
Pokémon Battle

Now that we have a grasp of how we can create our own custom types, we will expand upon it in this chapter. In this chapter, we will go through the following things:

- Creating a custom Pokémon type
- Creating instances of our Pokémon type and having them interact with each other
- Having *Charizard* and *Pikachu* fight with each other to solidify our understanding of having instances interact through the use of the methods that we create
- Having our Pokémon hug it out to help us understand how instances interact with each other

Pokémon type

When creating a program, there are times when you will want the instances of your various types to interact, in ways that allow them to communicate with each other (as in the real world). What does that mean exactly? Let's break it down.

To say we have an instance of a type means that we have an actual thing that can perform actions and respond to methods. It also has properties or attributes (hair color, eye color, and many more).

Let's start with a simple example and build on it as we progress through the chapter. Here's an example of a `Pokemon` class:

```
class Pokemon {
    let name: String
    init(name: String) {
        self.name = name
    }
}
```

 All related source code for this chapter can be found here: `https://githu b.com/swift-book-projects/swift-3-programming-for-kids/tree/ma ster/Chapter-10`

We've created a class called `Pokemon`. This means that we've created a brand new type that can be used anywhere throughout our iOS application (such as `String`, `Array`, or `Int`). This type can produce instances, which means that there can be instances of `Pokemon` running around out there in the world (if we so choose)! Each one can have its own name.

Let's create a new instance of `Pokemon` called `charizard` in the following line of code:

```
let charizard = Pokemon(name: "Charizard")
```

Here, `charizard` is a constant of the `Pokemon` type with the `name` property set to the value `Charizard`.

Let's create another instance of `Pokemon` called `pikachu`:

```
let pikachu = Pokemon(name: "Pikachu")
```

Here, `pikachu` is a constant of the `Pokemon` type with the `name` property set to the value `Pikachu`.

As you can see, `pikachu` and `charizard` are two separate instances of `Pokemon`.

Let's expand on this example a bit here. Let's add another instance property to our `Pokemon` type. We know that being a `Pokemon` means that you will have HP (Hit Points). It's a way of keeping track of your health. As you progress throughout the game and level up or evolve, your HP (Hit Points) will increase. Here, we are adding `hp` as a new instance property available to any instance of `Pokemon`:

```
class Pokemon {
    let name: String
    var hp: Int
```

```
init(name: String, hp: Int) {
    self.name = name
    self.hp = hp
}
}
```

We've added `hp` as a new property to our `Pokemon` type. Again, `hp` represents the Hit Points (health) that a `Pokemon` instance will have.

Let's go back and adjust how we created the preceding two instances of `Pokemon` to reflect this new `hp` property we've added:

```
let charizard = Pokemon(name: "Charizard", hp: 78)
let pikachu = Pokemon(name: "Pikachu", hp: 35)
```

Initializer syntax

In order to create an instance of any type, we need to use initializer syntax.

The initializer syntax is `()`. That's it, just an open and a closed parenthesis. Except they **need** to be typed *after* the end of a type. As in, type out the word `Pokemon`, since `Pokemon` is a type, and then open a parenthesis right after it, as shown here:

```
Pokemon(
```

As soon as you begin typing out something like that, you should note that autocomplete kicks in and the compiler tries to help you out. It should list all the options available to you that you can pick from (all the various initializers associated with that type). Here, we only have one:

This is really cool! Swift is helping us out here. By working with any type (`String`, `Int`, `Array`, and others.), not just our own custom types we made, we can begin to type out the parenthesis with an open parenthesis first to see what is available to us as autocomplete will kick in.

If we were to press the *return* key on our keyboard, we would now be met with the following code:

We can now fill in the blanks (name and hp). The compiler has now autocompleted the necessary fields for us to create an instance of a Pokemon. Now, we need to fill in those fields with the necessary information:

```
18 Pokemon(name: "Charizard", hp: 78)
```

There's one problem with this so far. We've correctly created an instance of a Pokemon, giving it the name Charizard along with a starting hp value of 78. However, we didn't store this value to a variable or constant. We have no way of referring back to this instance if we need to use it in our code later on. Let's fix that. Lets store this instance to a constant named charizard, as seen here:

```
18 let charizard = Pokemon(name: "Charizard", hp: 78)
```

This completes the puzzle (so far). Here is a screenshot of where we currently stand:

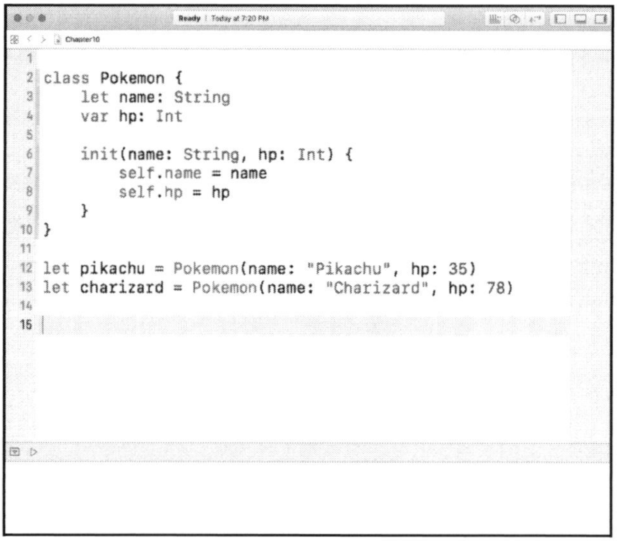

```
1
2 class Pokemon {
3     let name: String
4     var hp: Int
5
6     init(name: String, hp: Int) {
7         self.name = name
8         self.hp = hp
9     }
10 }
11
12 let pikachu = Pokemon(name: "Pikachu", hp: 35)
13 let charizard = Pokemon(name: "Charizard", hp: 78)
14
15 |
```

Functions and types

If we were to hold the *option* key and click either on the `pikachu` or `charizard` constant, the compiler would show us that it indeed is a constant (declared with the `let` keyword) of the `Pokemon` type as seen here:

Okay, so we understand that `pikachu` and `charizard` are both instances of the `Pokemon` type. Let's add two more instance properties to our `Pokemon` type: `attack` and `defense`. The code for this will be as illustrated:

```
class Pokemon {
    let name: String
    var hp: Int
    var attack: Int
    var defense: Int

    init(name: String, hp: Int, attack: Int, defense: Int) {
        self.name = name
        self.hp = hp
        self.attack = attack
        self.defense = defense
    }
}
```

Now our `Pokemon` type has four instance properties and one initializer.

Let's update how we're creating the preceding instances (for the last time, I promise!):

```
let pikachu = Pokemon(name: "Pikachu", hp: 35, attack: 55, defense: 40)
let charizard = Pokemon(name: "Charizard", hp: 78, attack: 84, defense: 78)
```

We can now write code like this:

```
if charizard.attack > pikachu.defense {
    print("Charizard can inflict damage.")
}
// Prints "Charizard can inflict damage."
```

`charizard.attack` is equal to `84` and `pikachu.defense` is equal to `40`. This evaluates to the following, if `84` is greater than `40` (which it is), we will enter the if-statement's first set of braces and execute any code within those braces. Here, we only have one `print` statement that executes and prints `Charizard can inflict damage.` to the console.

Let's do more with this. Let's create a function on the `Pokemon` type that allows us to interact with other instances of `Pokemon`:

```
func attack(pokemon: Pokemon) {
    if attack > pokemon.defense {
        let damage = attack - pokemon.defense
        pokemon.hp = pokemon.hp - damage
    }
}
```

Here we've created a function, `attack(pokemon:)` which takes in one argument labeled as `pokemon` of type `Pokemon`. It returns no values. We will step through the implementation of this function in the following section.

This function lives within our `Pokemon` class. This means that it's only available to be called on instances of `Pokemon` (such as `charizard` and `pikachu`). This is what our playground file currently looks like:

```
class Pokemon {
    let name: String
    var hp: Int
    var attack: Int
    var defense: Int

    init(name: String, hp: Int, attack: Int, defense: Int) {
        self.name = name
        self.hp = hp
        self.attack = attack
        self.defense = defense
    }

    func attack(pokemon: Pokemon) {
        if attack > pokemon.defense {
            let damage = attack - pokemon.defense
            pokemon.hp = pokemon.hp - damage
        }
    }
}

let pikachu = Pokemon(name: "Pikachu", hp: 35, attack: 55,
    defense: 40)

let charizard = Pokemon(name: "Charizard", hp: 78, attack: 84,
    defense: 78)
```

Before we go through the implementation of this `attack(pokemon:)` method, see if you can step through it yourself and solve the following problem. What will the following `print` statement print to the console? Ultimately, what is the remaining `hp` of `pikachu` after being passed along to the `attack(pokemon:)` function?:

```
charizard.attack(pokemon: pikachu)

print("Pikachu has (pikachu.hp) hit points.")
```

As a result of our call to the `attack(pokemon:)` method available to `charizard` being that `charizard` is an instance of `Pokemon`, we are giving this function what it wants, which is another instance of `Pokemon`. We're passing along to this function `pikachu` (which is another `Pokemon` instance). By calling on this method, we jump to the function itself and run through its implementation line by line with all of the necessary pieces in place.

We are now stepping through the implementation of `attack(pokemon:)`. Considering that `charizard` is the one who called on this method, anywhere we reference `attack` (within the implementation `attack(pokemon:)`), we are referring to the `charizard` instance's `attack` property because anytime you reference a variable or constant that is an instance property (such as `name`, `hp`, `attack`, or `defense`) within the scope of a function defined within the type, you are referring to the current instance's properties that called on that function. The `attack(pokemon:)` function takes in an argument of the `Pokemon` type labeled `pokemon`. Within the scope of this function, we have access to another constant, called `pokemon`, which is referring to the `Pokemon` instance that was passed to this function (which is `pikachu`). In our preceding example, we are passing the `pikachu` instance to this function, which means that, anywhere within the scope of that function, where we're typing things like `pokemon.defense` or `pokemon.hp`, we are referring to the `pikachu` instance's `defense` and `hp` because it was passed along to this function as an argument when `charizard` decided to call on this function. As a result, this is what our `print` statement will print to the console:

```
print("Pikachu has (pikachu.hp) hit points.")
// Prints "Pikachu has -9 hit points."
```

If you were to go through the preceding function, we would be left with `pikachu` having -9 hit points; a sad day for Pikachu.

Charizard versus pikachu

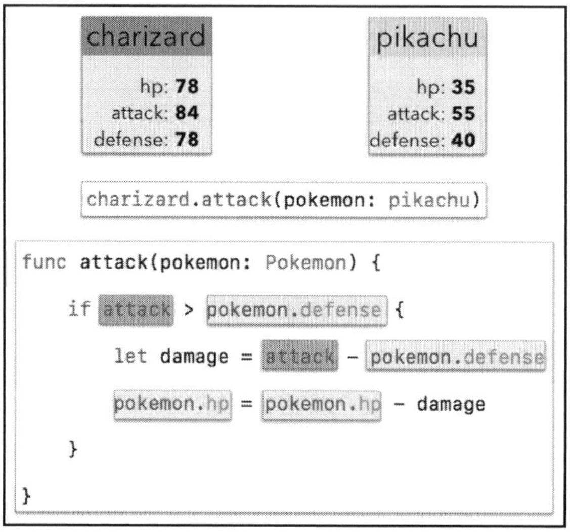

```
      charizard              pikachu

         hp: 78                 hp: 35
     attack: 84             attack: 55
    defense: 78            defense: 40


      charizard.attack(pokemon: pikachu)

func attack(pokemon: Pokemon) {

    if attack > pokemon.defense {

        let damage = attack - pokemon.defense

        pokemon.hp = pokemon.hp - damage

    }

}
```

If we replace all the code referring back to the caller's (`charizard`) instance properties, along with the argument's (`pikachu`) instance properties, we will be left with the following diagram:

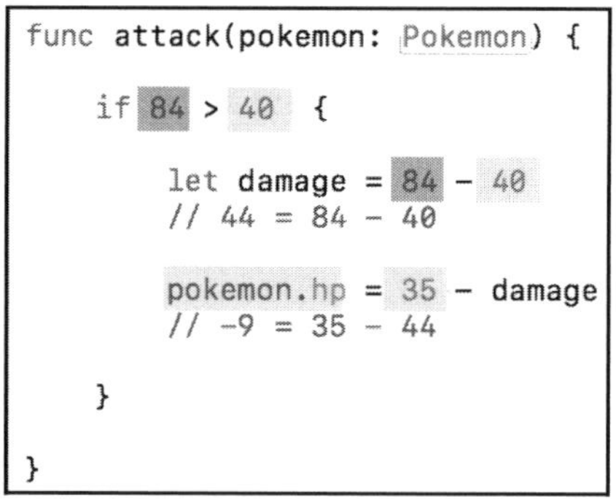

```
func attack(pokemon: Pokemon) {

    if 84 > 40 {

        let damage = 84 - 40
        // 44 = 84 - 40

        pokemon.hp = 35 - damage
        // -9 = 35 - 44

    }

}
```

As you can see, our `pikachu` instance is left standing with hit points less than zero (-9 to be exact).

Let's create a different scenario. Let's assume that the following line of code was run instead:

```
pikachu.attack(pokemon: charizard)

print("Charizard has (charizard.hp) hit points.")
// Prints "Charizard has 78 hit points."
```

Charizard's HP didn't go down; not even one point! That's because if you were to go through the function's implementation in the current scenario, we would never enter the if-statement. Similar to what we just did, make an attempt to go through the function yourself and try to replace the various references to instance properties in the scope of the function with the figures produced by the line of code that has `pikachu` attacking `charizard`. You should find right away that 55 (`pikachu` attack) is not greater than 78 (`charizard` defense) and that we will not enter the if-statement as 55 > 78 evaluates to `false`.

When creating functions within the `{}` braces of a custom type (such as `Pokemon`), those functions are only available to instances of that type. As you can see, in order to call on the `attack(pokemon:)` method, we first need an instance of the `Pokemon` type. That instance has the ability to call on methods only available to `Pokemon`. Currently, we have only this one method. When calling on this function (on an instance like `charizard` or `pikachu`), we know that it takes in one argument that is of the `Pokemon` type. This allows for the caller of this function (which would be any instance of `Pokemon`) to interact with another instance of `Pokemon` (as that is the argument of the function). Within the scope `{}` (braces of the function), we can have our instances interact with each other in any way we want. In this example, we had our instances fight in some capacity by checking to see what their instance properties are. Comparing the values of these instance properties, we will reduce the `hp` of the `Pokemon` instance passed in as an argument if the caller's `attack` exceeded the `defense` of the argument passed in.

Hug function

Let's create another function available to our `Pokemon` type:

```
func hug(pokemon: Pokemon) {
    if pokemon.name == "Pikachu" {
        hp = hp - 5
        print("Ouch!")
    } else {
        print("Thanks for the hug (pokemon.name).")
    }
}
```

This function, `hug(pokemon:)`, takes in an argument of the `Pokemon` type and returns no values. In our implementation, we are first checking to see if the `Pokemon` instance that is passed in as an argument to this function has the name `Pikachu`. If it does, then the `Pokemon` instance which called on this function will lose 5 `hp` along with us printing `Ouch!` to the console. We will enter the else-statement only if the if-statement evaluates to `false` (which would mean that the argument has a name other than `Pikachu`). If we enter the else-statement, we will print `Thanks for the hug x.` to the console, where the *x* (in this example) will be replaced with the name of the `Pokemon` instance that is passed in as an argument to the function.

Here's what our `Pokemon` type should look like right now:

```
class Pokemon {
    let name: String
    var hp: Int
    var attack: Int
    var defense: Int

    init(name: String, hp: Int, attack: Int, defense: Int) {
        self.name = name
        self.hp = hp
        self.attack = attack
        self.defense = defense
    }

    func attack(pokemon: Pokemon) {
        if attack > pokemon.defense  {
```

```
            let damage = attack - pokemon.defense
            pokemon.hp = pokemon.hp - damage
        }
    }

    func hug(pokemon: Pokemon) {
        if pokemon.name == "Pikachu" {
            hp = hp - 5
            print("Ouch!")
        } else {
            print("Thanks for the hug (pokemon.name).")
        }
    }

}
```

Let's also create a third `Pokemon` instance, named `Bulbasaur`. This will leave us with the following code:

```
let pikachu = Pokemon(name: "Pikachu", hp: 35, attack: 55, defense: 40)

let charizard = Pokemon(name: "Charizard", hp: 78, attack: 84, defense: 78)

let bulbasaur = Pokemon(name: "Bulbasaur", hp: 45, attack: 49, defense: 49)
```

What will happen if we write the following line of code in our playground file:

```
bulbasaur.hug(pokemon: charizard)
```

Go through our implementation of the preceding function and see if you can figure out exactly what happens and what prints to the console. After giving it a shot, you should find that the following output is what prints to the console:

```
Thanks for the hug Charizard.
```

That's awesome! Instead of fighting, our Pokémon are now getting along. The caller of this function was `bulbasaur`, which is an instance of `Pokemon` (which is why it can call on the `hug(pokemon:)` method). Passed along as an argument to this function was `charizard` (which is a separate instance of `Pokemon`).

Now, when going through our implementation of the `hug(pokemon:)` function, anywhere where we reference the `pokemon` constant (which is the name of the parameter), we are instead referring to our `charizard` instance. Considering all of that, we will end up getting to the following line of code:

```
print("Thanks for the hug (pokemon.name).")
```

`Thanks for the hug Charizard` is what prints to the console because `pokemon.name` will return because we are accessing the `charizard` instance's `name` property.

Let's try having `charizard` hug `pikachu` and see what happens. He will get zapped! At all costs, you should avoid hugging Pikachu.

Step through the following code to see if you can understand what's going on:

```
charizard.hug(pokemon: pikachu)
// Prints "Ouch!"
```

As we can see, `Ouch!` is what prints to the console. This seems easy enough, but what happened to `charizard` Hit Points (`hp`)? It went down by 5. Take a look at the following print statement:

```
print("Charizard has (charizard.hp) hit points remaining.")
// Prints "Charizard has 73 hit points remaining.
```

Charizard started with 78 Hit Points. It now has 73 Hit Points because it tried to hug `pikachu`, which we know is a big mistake (never hug Pikachu!).

Summary

This chapter had Pokémon fighting and hugging. One of the most important lessons we learned was that you shouldn't hug Pikachu. This chapter helped you learn how to create your own custom types and create functions to have instances of your custom type interact with other instances of the same type.

The next chapter will introduce you to **Interface Builder**. We will now be stepping into one of the more exciting areas of iOS development, which is designing what your application will look like and how it will feel in the hands of someone else.

11
Simon Says

Until now, the programs we have written have been focused on text; they have been console applications as described in `Chapter 3`, *Say Hello*. A very central part of an iPhone application is the **User Interface** (**UI**)–the interface in which the user is able to do gestures, such as drag, force-touch, swipe, and more; the interface in which the user is able to communicate back and forth with the running application.

The following two chapters will focus on the UI in an iOS application. The reader will acquire the necessary knowledge and skills in order to be able to write programs that leverage a UI. To summarize, this chapter will cover the following topics:

- A recap of the concept of a **Graphical User Interface** (**GUI**)
- A guide to setting up a new iOS project that will include a UI
- An introduction to how we can lay out a view using Xcode's built-in tool **Interface Builder** (**IB**) and something called **storyboards**
- A guide to building a small application called *Simon Says*, that uses a GUI

GUI

Before going into detail about how to create a UI for our applications, let's remember what a GUI is? You might remember how we introduced two different kinds of interfaces in Chapter 3, *Say Hello*: a console interface and a GUI. While a console application is very much focused around text when communicating with a user, a GUI leverages on the fact that we have screens on most electronic devices, for example, your TV:

More or less every TV today ships with a GUI that you can use to adjust your settings, such as the sound level or the level of brightness on your TV. Newer TVs, so-called *Smart TVs*, also ship with a lot of features, such as a web browser and access to Netflix and HBO. You usually interact with your TV using your remote control. The TV gives you feedback on your choices or commands using the remote through sound or by visually updating what you see on the TV.

A GUI is about interacting with the user using visuals. These visuals can be items such as windows, buttons, sliders, icons, and menus and are present in most operating systems, such as the systems you use when using an iPhone, iMac, or a computer running the Windows operating system.

Laying out a view

In order to make a GUI, we need a strategy. For example, how do we control that a certain button should have the red color? How do we ensure that the background color changes when the user taps on the button? How do we position our different UI elements so that they look reasonable across different devices with different screen sizes, such as the iPhone and iPad? In order to answer all these questions, we need a way to control the UI. Apple offers us some tools and patterns that have been developed over time. Some of the concepts are similar to other platforms and some are specific when you develop applications for Apple devices.

Setting up a new iOS project

IB is a tool offered as part of Xcode. It is a tool for designing and laying out a UI. It helps the creator visualize what the interface will look like when running the application and also enables faster prototyping when a UI is needed.

Go ahead and open Xcode if it is not already open. If you see the welcome view, then go ahead and click on **Create a new Xcode project** or navigate to **File | New | Project...**. The next step will be to choose a template for our new project. For this small application, ensure that the **Single View Application** is selected and then click on **Next**:

In the next step of the wizard, you will be able to type in some information about the project:

- **Product Name**: This will be the name of the application. For this project, type in **Simon Says**.
- **Team**: This is related to the distribution of the application, which is not relevant now; choose **None**.
- **Organization Name**: This requires your name to be typed in.
- **Organization Identifier**: This is also related to the distribution of the application, which is not relevant now. For now, type in `com.yourname`, where `yourname` is without any space or special characters.
- **Language**: For this, ensure that **Swift** is selected.
- **Devices**: For this, choose **iPhone**.
- Ensure that the **Use Core Data**, **Include Unit Tests**, and **Include UI Tests** checkboxes remain unchecked:

Click on **Next** and find a spot on your computer to save your new project. Remember to put it in a place where will be able to locate it again. Then, Xcode should have automatically opened your newly created project and you should see something like this:

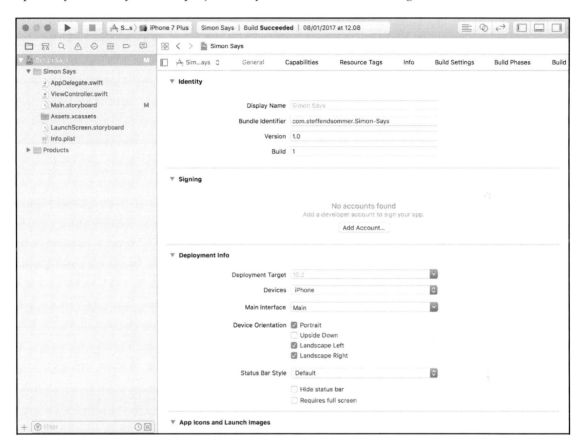

Although this might seem a bit overwhelming, don't worry, we will take it step-by-step. First up, let's take a look at the toolbar placed at the top of the window. To the left, we have the play and stop buttons for running and stopping our application.

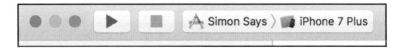

Next, we have the name of our application, followed by the type of device that should run our application (which is the target we want to run). Clicking on the device type brings forward a small menu where all the different iOS simulators can be selected.

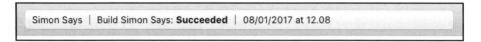

To the right, we have two groups of controls: the first one lets you configure the editor area and the second one hides/shows the different areas of Xcode. Go ahead and press the three different buttons to the far right of the toolbar to toggle the different areas of Xcode. This is very similar to what we saw when using playgrounds.

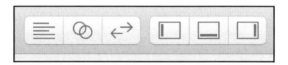

Below the toolbar, we have the different areas of Xcode. Go ahead and toggle all the areas to be able to get an overview of the different parts of Xcode. Also, to be able to see the source editor, click on the `AppDelegate.swift` file on the left to have it opened in the source editor:

To the left, we have the **Navigator**, which we will mainly use to browse the different files in our project. As you might have noted, Xcode has already added a few files to our newly created project– in the middle, we have the source editor where we will be writing the code for our program; on the right, we have the **Utilities** area that is split in two: one part for inspecting the different elements of our project and one part for having a library of elements we can add to our project; at the bottom, we have the **Debug** area that includes a console, which we already learned how to print to.

Xcode's Interface Builder and storyboards

One of the newer approaches to laying out views in Xcode is to use **storyboards**. We can think of storyboards as our canvas for designing the different views in our application. Storyboards are very powerful and offer more than just the laying out of views. Another central feature they offer is handling navigation flow; that is, when you click on a profile picture in an app, the app can navigate to the profile view.

For now, let's focus on how to lay out a UI in Xcode. If you look to the left of Xcode, in the Navigator area, you should see the following files:

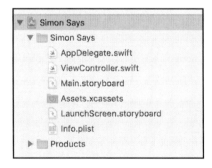

If we go through the files Xcode already created for us, we can see that there are already two `.storyboard` files: one named `Main.storyboard` and one named `LaunchScreen.storyboard`. The launch screen is a special kind of view that will be shown immediately when you open your application, while the application is loading. The storyboard we are most interested in at this point is the `Main.storyboard`, so go ahead and click on that file to let IB open the storyboard file:

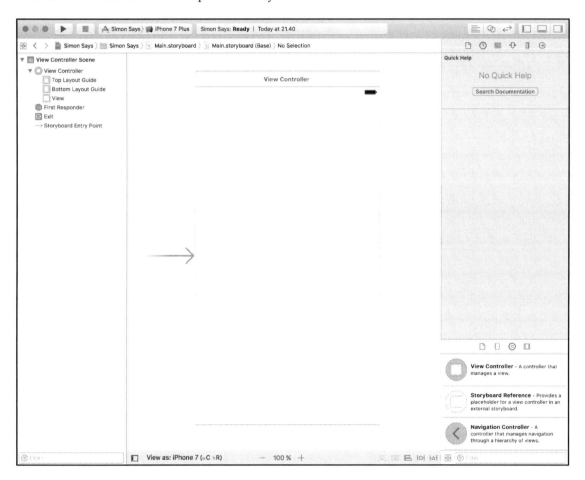

 All related source code for this chapter can be found here: `https://github.com/swift-book-projects/swift-3-programming-for-kids/tree/master/Chapter-11`

This is our canvas for laying out our UI. If we run our application now (using the play control at the top-left corner of Xcode), we will see this white canvas in the simulator. On the left-hand side of Xcode, we see the **Outline** view that will give us a list of views once we start adding them to our canvas. The way the views are listed corresponds to how they are present in the view hierarchy, which will be explained in the following chapter (Chapter 12, *Starry Night*). On the right-hand side of Xcode, we have the Utilities area that now contains a list of elements that we are able to drag and drop to our canvas:

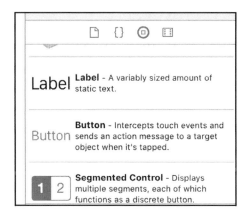

If you scroll down the list, you will begin noticing elements such as **Label**, **Button**, and **Text Field**, which are some of the UI elements we can use for our interface. Feel free to try and drag a button to the center of our canvas.

After dropping it to the canvas, it should automatically be selected and some options in the Utilities area should be visible now:

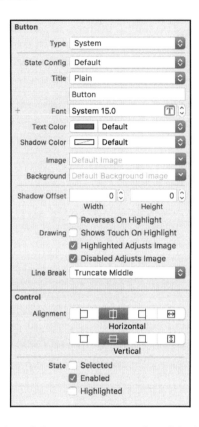

This area will now let us do a lot of things to our newly added button, such as changing the visible label on the button, the colors, the font, and a lot more. In the Outline view on the left, the button should now appear on the list of UI elements under **View**:

In terms of defining our views in relation to each other, we can see that our button became a subview or a child of **View**, which in this case is the main view. We can see that by how the button is indented below the main view.

Simon says

It is time to use our knowledge about laying out interface elements on our canvas using the Xcode's IB by creating a small application. We will try to make a small *Simon Says* application, which will not be fully functional, but will have an interface that is similar to a fully working *Simon Says* app:

A *Simon Says* application is a simple memory game where the user has to memorize an increasing number of color combinations. Basically, the user takes turns with the application and tries to mimic the colors the application has chosen. For example, if the app starts out by choosing blue, then the user should, afterwards, press the blue button. Then, the application will repeat the already-chosen color blue and then choose a new color, for example, red. Then, the user should press the blue button, followed by the red button. This pattern continues until the user is unable to remember the right combination of colors.

Designing the interface

For this small application, we will use the Xcode project we already created (and named *Simon Says*). Let's open up `Main.storyboard` and delete the button we already added to ensure that we start from scratch. You can delete the button by selecting it and then pressing *Backspace*.

Then, we will drag four plain views onto the canvas; one for each corner. The view is called **View** in the list and can be found towards the bottom:

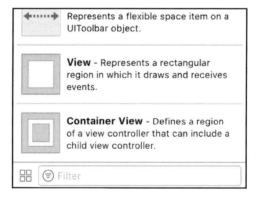

Then, by selecting each of the views individually, we are able to set the background color of the button in the Utilities area on the right. For each button on the canvas, we will apply a different background color, such as green, red, yellow, or blue. If the specific color you want does not appear on the list, you can click on **Other** at the bottom of the dropdown to select another color using a color picker:

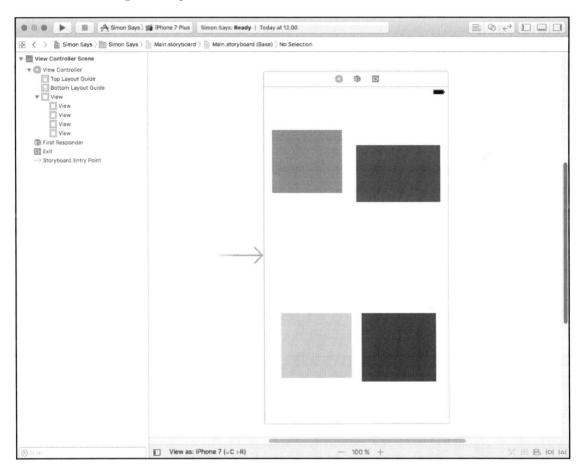

Having four views on the canvas, one for each corner, we will make them fill up approximately 25% of the screen each, by positioning the views and dragging their corners in order to resize them:

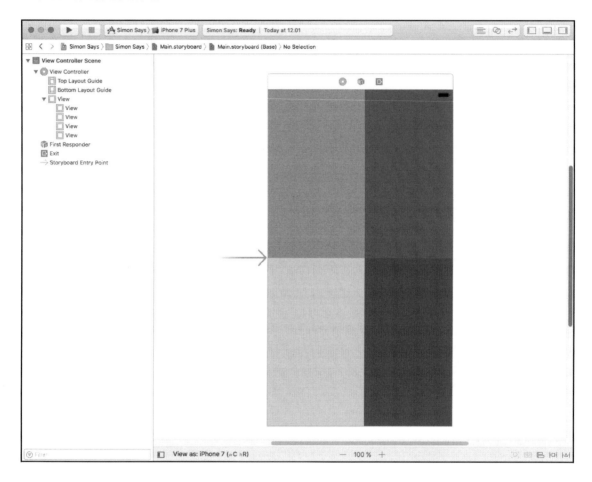

If we take a look at the bottom of the IB, it should say something like **View as: iPhone 7,** which means that the canvas we have been using to design our interface has been based on the screen size of an iPhone 7. If we now ensure that we select the iPhone 7 as the device for our simulator (close to the play/run button), we should be able to see our interface as we have designed it:

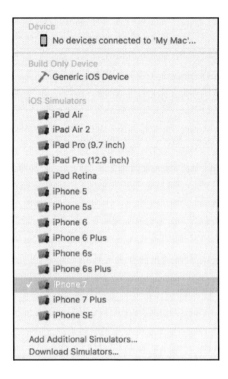

Running the application will open up the simulator and the interface should look similar to how we designed it:

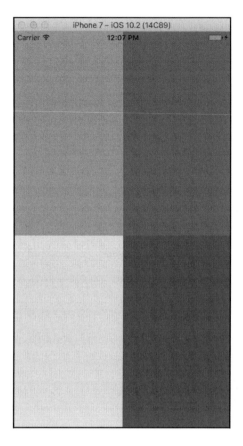

This is quite exciting, as we have now designed our very own UI. It is running on a simulator (which mimics a real device), and is looking as we designed it. Good job!

The way we designed our interface using Xcode's IB was fairly straightforward, as we basically just dragged and dropped the elements we wanted to have in our interface and, afterwards, repositioned them to our needs. However, there is a bit more work to making a UI that will scale across devices with different screen sizes. If we try to run our application on an iPhone 7 Plus opposed to the iPhone 7, we should see the following view:

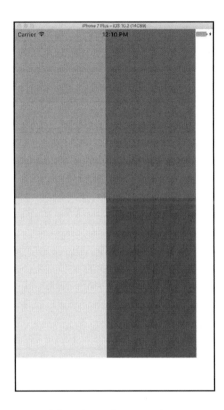

This shows that the UI we designed for the iPhone 7 does not scale as the size of the screen grows. To fix this, we need to look at other strategies for laying out a view, which will be covered in the next chapter.

Summary

This chapter introduced GUI and how we can construct a GUI using Xcode's IB. It started out by guiding us on how to set up a new Xcode project that includes a UI. Next, we introduced the IB, which is a tool for laying out views and is bundled together with Xcode. Using that tool, we looked at how to lay out a view on a storyboard.

We ended the chapter using all the acquired knowledge to create a small *Simon Says* application. The interface includes multiple views with different colors and the idea of the application was to simulate a *Simon Says* game. We briefly looked at how the interface we created did not scale well across devices with different screen sizes.

In the next chapter, we will dive even further into GUI and look at how we can make user interfaces scale better. We will also be building a small application that will let the user click on buttons to animate the background of the application.

12
Starry Night

Continuing with what we learned in the last chapter, in this chapter, we will take a closer look at how GUIs can be made for iOS. We will go through the central concepts of UI and start looking at how we can bridge the gap between UI and the code we write using the Swift programming language.

We will finish the chapter by making a small application that will be able to handle user input and, based on that, change the colors of the background. To make it even more cool, we will change the colors using animation. In other words, we will be doing the following things:

- Looking at the fundamental concepts of UI, such as view hierarchy, frames, bounds, and **Auto Layout**
- Looking at the view life cycle that will make it easier for developers to know the state of the app
- Making a small application where we will tie our UI with some code that we will write to change the background color of our application

A deep dive into UI in iOS

In Chapter 11, *Simon Says*, we created a simple UI with four subviews, each representing a color in the *Simon Says* memory game. Toward the end of the chapter, we tried to run our application on a device with a different screen size and noted how our UI elements did not scale and the interface ended up looking different from how we wanted it to look. In this section, we will dive deeper into how GUI works in order to come up with a better strategy to lay out our UI.

The view hierarchy

A UI in iOS is built using something we refer to as views. A view represents an element, such as an icon, menu, text field, or a button. A view can have multiple child views or subviews and a view can have one parent view. Let's illustrate this with a simple example:

This UI is supposed to look like a chat interface, where the user of the app is able to write messages back and forth with **John**. Let's go through the different UI elements:

- Profile section, which is the blue area at the top
- Profile image
- Profile name
- Profile occupation
- Message section, which is the white area that takes up most of the view
- Message log headline
- A label showing the last written message
- Text field to write messages
- Button to submit messages

When you look at the UI and argue how the different elements are placed or laid out in the app, it is reasonable to say that the profile section (the blue area) contains other UI elements, such as the profile picture, profile name, and occupation. If we imagine the UI being in a 3D space, we can see that those elements are placed on top of the blue area. We can also say that the **Message log** title and the last written chat message (**Me: Hi John, how are you doing?**) has the same parent view and neither contains any other views.

This is very similar to how we describe view hierarchies in iOS–when we lay out the views in the UI of an iOS app, we do it using view hierarchies. This means that each view (for instance, an image or a label) has one parent view, but can potentially have multiple child or subviews, with the exception of the view that we can refer to as the **main view**. The main view is the view that defines the bounds of our application, which means that it defines the size of our application. This will vary depending on which Apple device we target when we write our iOS application. The main view will not have any parent view as it is the lowest or the first view in the hierarchy.

All the other views will have one parent view (we say that it is placed inside the parent view) and can have none or multiple subviews. Xcode has a feature to debug the view hierarchy, which will give us this representation of our user interface:

If you want to use this tool for one of your applications, you will then have to open Interface Builder, for example, by opening a .storyboard file. Then while your application is running, a bar at the bottom of Interface Builder will appear. Clicking on the two rectangles with the name **Debug View Hierarchy** will open up the tool.

Using this tool, we can see how elements are placed in a 3D space where views are contained (placed on top of) on other views. If we look at our list of UI elements, we can now write this in a slightly different way according to the preceding screenshot:

- Main view
    - Profile section, which is the blue area at the top
        - Profile image
        - Profile name
        - Profile occupation
    - Message section, which is the white area that takes up most of the view
    - Message log headline
    - A label showing the last written message
    - Text field to write messages
    - Button to submit messages

This means that we have a main view that does not have any parent and that has multiple subviews. These subviews include the profile section that also has its own subviews, such as the profile image. The main view also has other subviews, such as the message log title and the last written chat message. The text field and button at the bottom look like they have multiple views, but this is due to some technical details that are not important at this point.

Frames and bounds

We have now seen how elements are placed in a UI using a hierarchy of views. The next step is to look at how elements are placed in the 2D space, that is, how do we size views and how do we place them according to the bounds of the main view.

We lay out views in iOS using a coordinate system. The coordinate system has its origin in the top-left corner of the screen and we refer to this point as 0,0. The horizontal axis of the coordinate system is labelled with *X* and the vertical axis of the coordinate system is labelled with *Y*. This means that *(X, Y) = (5, 10)* refers to a point on the screen found by counting 5 points from the left of the screen toward right and by counting 10 points from the top of the screen toward the bottom:

A size refers to the amount of points a view should take up on the screen. A size is defined as having a width and a height. The combination of a view's location (using a point in the coordination system) and the size of a view gives us the view's `frame`. We say that a view's frame describes a view's location and size in relation to its parent's view coordinate system. In the preceding example interface, we lay out the profile section (the blue area) according to the main view (the bounds of the screen with a white background). The profile picture, however, is laid out according to the profile section. This means that if we change the position of the profile section, all its subviews will follow, which also seems intuitive if we think of the profile section containing its subviews.

We refer to locations and sizes in our coordinate system in points instead of pixels. As the pixel density of iOS device screens increases, it becomes harder to align interfaces across devices with different pixel density. A view placed in our interface and defined in pixels will look smaller and smaller if run on devices with higher and higher pixel density. To avoid having to deal with resizing, we use points instead and let the iOS do it for us.

Bounds, on the other hand, refers to the location and size of a view in relation to its own coordination system (opposed to its parent coordination system). We've already referred to the bounds of the screen as being the canvas for where we can draw and lay out views for our UI. This means that the bounds of our profile section describe the canvas for where any subview is able to lay out views. This means that when we add a profile picture as a subview to the profile section, the bounds of the profile section define how we can position our profile picture.

Auto Layout

In the early days of iOS programming, laying out UI using frames and bounds was easy and commonly used by programmers. Laying out views using frames and bounds is somewhat intuitive and it is fairly easy to use Xcode's visual tools to drag and drop UI elements into a view. However, with the rise of additional iOS devices with different screen sizes, the approach of using frames and bounds became difficult. As the screen dimension could now be very different depending on if it was an iPhone 7 or an iPad that was running the application, one had to do a lot of view calculations in order to scale a view. Let's illustrate this example by looking at the UI we created earlier. This is how it looked on an iPhone 7:

Let's see how this view looks on an iPhone 7 Plus:

What just happened? We took the same view that looked fine on the iPhone 7 and tried to run it on an iPhone 7 Plus that has a bigger screen and, for some reason, the interface now looks odd. There is some extra white space on the right and at the bottom of the screen, which was not the case on the iPhone 7.

It is not by coincidence that the origin of the screen's coordinate system is at the top-left corner of the screen and the white space that appears after running the app (on an iPhone 7 Plus) is visible on the right side and at the bottom of the screen. This example points exactly to the limitation of laying out views using frames and bounds, that is, one needs to calculate where to position views if the screen size or rotation changes. In this example, we placed the profile section at the top-left corner of the main view and gave it a fixed height and width that aligned it with the bounds of the iPhone 7. When we lay out the same view on a different screen size, for example, the iPhone 7 Plus, the view will look different.

This is why Apple introduced Auto Layout. It lets us design interfaces in a relative manner, which makes it more flexible and generic, as opposed to being fixed. Basically, the way Auto Layout works in is that you set up a set of constraints. Then, when the application is running, the device will try to satisfy these constraints whether the orientation of the device changes or the same application is being run on another device with a different screen size. Here are a couple of examples of constraints that can be made using Auto Layout:

- Distance from a view's edge (being top, bottom, left, or right) to another view's edge
- The width/height of a view in relation to the width/height of another view
- Center a view horizontally/vertically inside its parent view

Let's consider the top part of our interface, the profile section:

We clearly have a problem with the width of our profile section now that the width of the screen size has increased (going from iPhone 7 to iPhone 7 Plus). Instead of setting a fixed size of the profile section, let's try to express it in a relative manner. We can say that we want our profile section (the blue area) to have 0 points of distance from the left and right edge to its parent view (the main view). This will mean that even though the width of the screen changes, the profile section will always just align with the right and left edges of the screen. In other words, it will fill up the horizontal space. How do we express the height in a relative manner? One approach can be to use the same technique as we just did with the width, but then introducing x points of spacing from the bottom of our profile section to the bottom of the screen; this means that if the height of the screen grows, the profile section also grows in height and vice versa; however, the tricky part is to define this value for the number of points we need for spacing. Another approach can be to have the height of the profile section proportional to the height of the screen.

This will make the relationship between the profile section and the screen more flexible in the sense that we directly express the proportional size relationship without having to know anything about the expected height. Adding these two constraints will make our interface look a little better:

Right now, the profile section's height will be 30% of the height of the screen size. This means that as the height of the device changes, the profile section's height will proportionally follow. The next step will be to ensure that the profile picture, name, and occupation will align correctly inside the profile section even though the size of the profile section will change. However, for introducing Auto Layout and the general principle of wanting to express the layout in a relative manner, this is fine for now.

The UIViewController life cycle

As the requirements for our UI grow, we need to have more granular control of our views. We need to be able to tell what *state* our view is currently in inside our code. Is it, for example, shown or did the user just close the app? Is the app currently navigating from one view to another or is it just about to be shown, but still loading. All of these states refer to the **life cycle** of the UIViewController, which is very important when we want to build a great UI. The life cycle of a view can be overwhelming to dive into, but often we only need a couple of these states in order to make our UIs as we want them to be. The way we handle these states is by implementing certain methods defined by Apple. Then, Apple guarantees to call these methods at the right moment according to the view life cycle. Let's take a look at some of the important states related to the UIViewController:

- viewDidLoad(): This method will be called after a view has been loaded and is about to be shown. This state is useful for setting up any initialization or configuration that needs to be set in code opposed to the storyboard.
- viewWillAppear(_:): This method will be called after viewDidLoad(), right before the view is shown to the user. This state is useful for reloading data or doing last-minute view setup. It is important to know that this state can be triggered multiple times if the user takes an application back and forth from the background (without leaving this view). This is different from viewDidLoad(), which in this case will be called only once (the first time the view gets loaded).
- viewDidAppear(_:): This method will be called after viewWillAppear(_:), right after the view has become visible to the user. This state is useful for firing off animations as soon as the user is able to see the view.
- viewWillDisappear(_:): This method will be called sometime after viewDidAppear(_:), right before the view is hidden from the user. This can be due to the user navigating further in the application flow or putting the app in the background.

Starry Night

We have covered a lot of fundamental concepts related to UIs in iOS in this chapter, and it is now time to use that knowledge to create a small application. We will create an application named *Starry Night*, which is a simple application that will animate the background of the application based on input from the user. Specifically, the user will be able to press two buttons: *Day* and *Night*; we will animate the background based on that.

Designing the UI

Using the same approach as explained in `Chapter 11`, *Simon Says*, we will create a new
(**Single View Application**) project that we name *Starry Night*. Remember to save the project
on a place on your hard drive where you will be able to locate it again.

Next, we will open up `Main.storyboard` and drag two buttons onto our canvas toward
the bottom.

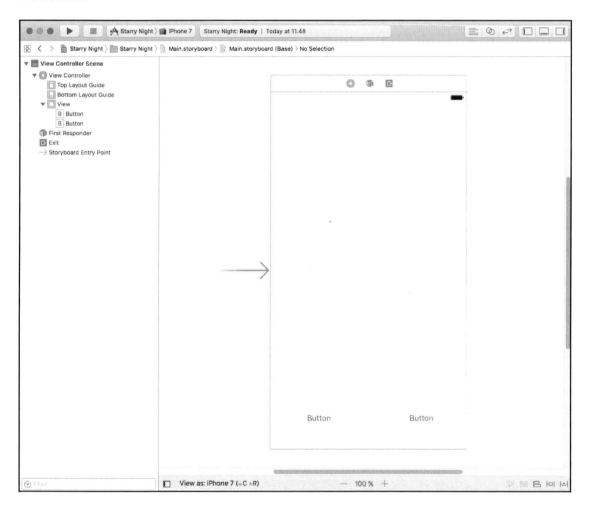

All related source code for this chapter can be found here: `https://github.com/swift-book-projects/swift-3-programming-for-kids/tree/master/Chapter-12`

Then, we will name the button on the left `Day` and the button on the right `Night`. You can rename the button by double-clicking on the button on the canvas or using the inspector on the right side of Xcode, as can be seen in the following screenshot, where we just named our button `Night`:

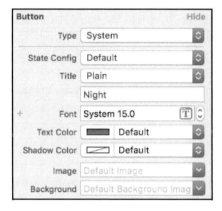

With that in place, we need to set up the **Auto Layout** constraints to ensure that our interface scales correctly when being run on devices with different screen sizes. Start by selecting the button with the name Day in the lower-left corner. Then, after it has been selected, click on the small square icon at the bottom:

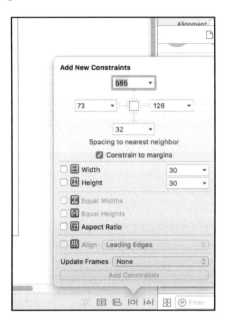

Clicking on that icon will bring up a small window that will assist us in adding some constraints.

The first part of the window that has a small square symbol with values on each side makes it easy for us to add constraints for our button, which will tell it how to be positioned in relation to its nearest neighbors in the view hierarchy. In this case, we are interested in ensuring that it will pin to the bottom and to the left, offset by 25 points. To do this, we enter 25 in the field to the left and to the bottom of the square. Note how the red lines become solid as we enter values, indicating that our constraint is now active on those sides of our view:

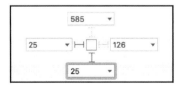

Having pinned the button to the lower-left corner, we need to specify the size of our button. Luckily for us, **Interface Builder (IB)** has already filled in its current size, which should match the size of the name we added for our button. All we need to do is activate these constraints. To do this, we just check the two checkboxes for **Width** and **Height**. Lastly, we select the **Items of New Constraints** option for **Update Frames** to ensure that the position of our button will be updated on the canvas. This will make it a little easier for us to validate that the constraints we just added correspond to how we imagined the position of our button. All the constraints for the *Day* button should look like this:

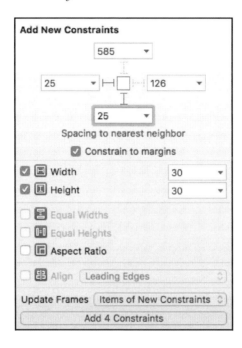

After clicking on **Add Constraints**, your canvas should look something like this:

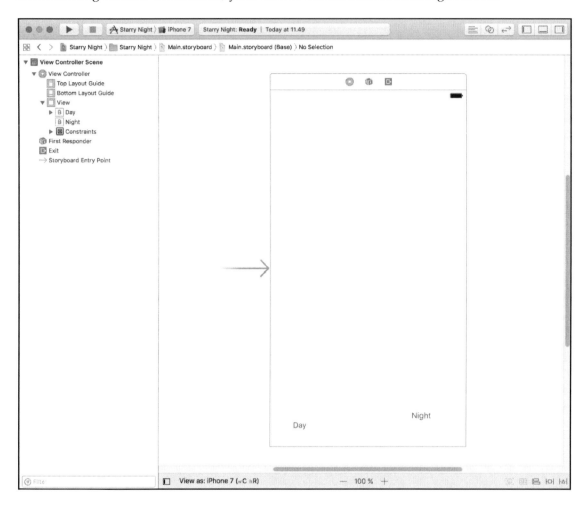

Now we will do the same thing for the button on the right named `Night` but, in this case, we will make it pin the right-hand side and the bottom of the square. This means that the constraints to add should look as follows:

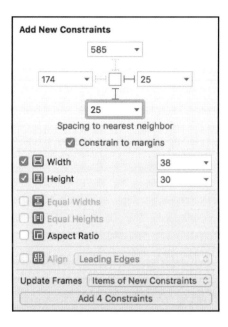

Note how the values for **Width** and **Height** in this case are not equal as the name of this button is longer. Then, try to run the application on an iPhone 7 and ensure that our buttons are positioned correctly toward the corners at the bottom:

In order to validate that our UI scales correctly across devices with different screen sizes, let's try to run it on an iPhone 7 Plus as well. If the constraints have been set up correctly, it should look great. Our interface now scales with the size of the screen. Instead of adding extra white space on the right-hand side and at the bottom, our interface now looks similar to how we designed it for iPhone 7.

Adding functionality to our interface

In the earlier chapters, we programmed console applications using playgrounds and in the previous chapter, we started looking at how we can use IB in Xcode to lay out views. The last but most important part is how we tie the two worlds together, that is, how do we write code that can be triggered by the click of a button? How do we update the background color of our view when something happens in our code? The glue between these two worlds is something called a **View Controller**, which has the UIViewController type.

 When writing iOS applications, and software in general, we often use patterns that tells us how to organize our code as well as how the different parts should communicate. When writing iOS application, a pattern called Model-View-Controller (often referred to as MVC) is very popular. The details of this pattern is outside the scope of this book, but we encourage any interested reader to read up on this.

The UIViewController is a special type that can be tied together with a view (the canvas we looked at) in a storyboard. This enables our app to communicate back and forth between the view and our code. Before looking into how to do this, open up the ViewController.swift and simplify its content by removing some methods so that you end up with the following code:

```
import UIKit

class ViewController: UIViewController {

}
```

Next, we will open Main.storyboard again and then make Xcode show the **Assistant editor** by clicking on the icon with two circles in the top-right corner of Xcode:

This should give you two vertically divided source editors. The one on the left should be the storyboard we already selected and the one on the right should automatically be the `ViewController.swift` file. If not, ensure that you set it to automatic at the top of the right source editor so that it selects this file automatically:

Having these two views side by side, we are now able to connect the two. Press and hold *Ctrl* while holding the left-click on the button named **Day** in the canvas. Then, while holding the left-click and beginning from the button, dragging into the editor on the right-hand side in the view controller and let go when inside the class body:

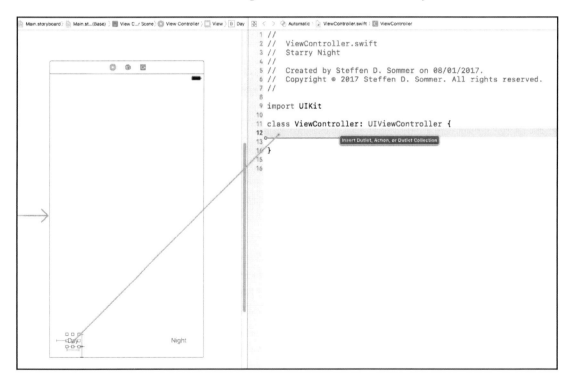

If done right, this should give you a small popup, which lets you define the connection we are about to make. In that popup, we will set the **Connection** to **Action** and type in **dayTapped** as the name of our action:

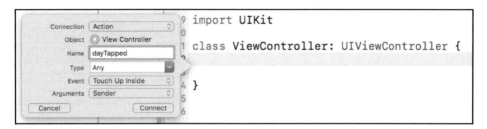

After pressing **Connect**, Xcode should generate some code for the view controller class so that you will end up with the following:

```
import UIKit

class ViewController: UIViewController {

    @IBAction func dayTapped(_ sender: Any) {
    }

}
```

This means that when we tap on our Day button, this function, named `dayTapped`, will be called. We will now do the same thing for the Night button so that we end up with two functions inside our class body. Let's call the second function `nightTapped` and remember to set the **Connection** to **Action**. Your `ViewController.swift` should now look like this:

```
import UIKit

class ViewController: UIViewController {

    @IBAction func dayTapped(_ sender: Any) {
    }

    @IBAction func nightTapped(_ sender: Any) {
    }
}
```

Now that we have a place to put code that will be called, we can add our animation code, which will take care of animating the background when pressing the buttons. To do this, we will make a small `UIView` animation where we will specify the duration of the animation and the actual work involved in the animation. For our `dayTapped` function, we can add the following:

```
UIView.animate(withDuration: 1, animations: {
    self.view.backgroundColor = UIColor(red: 0.64, green: 0.83, blue: 0.93,
alpha: 1)
})
```

In the preceding code, we say that the animation should take exactly one second to perform, and the animation itself involves changing the background color to a light blue color. We can do the same for the `nightTapped` button, but in this animation we will use the another `UIColor: UIColor(red: 0, green: 0, blue: 0.20, alpha: 1)`, which will give us a nice dark blue color.

`ViewController.swift` should now contain the following code:

```
import UIKit

class ViewController: UIViewController {

    @IBAction func dayTapped(_ sender: Any) {
        UIView.animate(withDuration: 1, animations: {
            self.view.backgroundColor = UIColor(red: 0.64, green: 0.83,
blue: 0.93, alpha: 1)
        })
    }

    @IBAction func nightTapped(_ sender: Any) {
        UIView.animate(withDuration: 1, animations: {
            self.view.backgroundColor = UIColor(red: 0, green: 0, blue:
0.20, alpha: 1)
        })
    }
}
```

If you run the application and try to press the buttons with the labels **Day** and **Night**, you will see that it will animate between the colors we specified in our code:

Summary

This chapter covered a lot of ground related to how interfaces work and how we can construct them using Xcode's Interface Builder. The chapter started out by explaining the view hierarchy and how we can use that to position elements using frames, bounds, and Auto Layout. We also briefly looked at some of the important states in the view life cycle:

- `viewDidLoad()`: This is called after the view has been loaded
- `viewWillAppear(_:)`: This is called every time the view is about to appear to the user

- `viewDidAppear(_:)`: This is called every time the view appears to the user
- `viewWillDisappear(_:)`: This is called every time the view is about to disappear for the user

We ended the chapter by making a small application, which we called *Starry Night*. The application scaled correctly across devices with different screen sizes because we used Auto Layout constraints. The application was able to animate the background color based on the user tapping the buttons. The application also showed how to tie the UI together with the code we write in our view controllers.

In the next chapter, we will continue to build user interfaces and start adding more code to our application, making it more fun and engaging to use.

13
Space Pizza Delivery

In this chapter, we will build a fully featured iOS application. We will begin by designing our own custom classes, along with learning what enumerations are and how we can take advantage of them when building our apps.

We will create a Space Pizza Delivery iOS Application. We will go step by step from creating an Xcode project, to writing the necessary code to make our application function. We will be covering the following topics:

- Enumerations
- Private variables
- Property observers
- Protocols
- UIPickerView
- Switch statements

Space Pizza

Let's assume that we're in some distant future that allows us to travel at the speed of light. Not only that, as a species, we've been able to figure out a way to inhabit all the planets in our solar system. This was no small feat! Our great great grandfather (named Frank) used to run his own pizza shop in our hometown on Earth, Brooklyn. Out of respect for him, we've decided to create the very first inter galactic pizza delivery service and call it Frank's Pizza.

In this distant future, everyone's love of pizza still exists. Due to this, our pizza service can deliver pizza to any planet in our solar system.

However, there's one problem. Traveling to these planets isn't cheap, so we've decided to create the following flyer to let everyone know what the costs are for getting a homemade slice of Brooklyn pizza delivered to them. Here is the flyer we've made which we intend to hand out to everyone:

After completing this iOS application, you will note that the prices on this flyer don't reflect the actual prices we charge for delivering pizza to these planets in our app. This is because this is a promotional flyer and the prices reflected here were available for a limited time only.

Xcode

The following is a screenshot of the iOS application you will be building in this chapter:

This iOS application will help us determine the delivery cost for delivering pizza to a certain planet. We will shortly go into detail as to what space junk is. When running the app, we will be able to scroll through our list of planets so that we can choose which one we want to deliver pizza to. We will also be able to change the space junk level by tapping on one of the three buttons (low, medium, or high). After selecting both the planet and the space junk level, we will update our label to reflect the pizza delivery cost.

Create a new Xcode application (**Single View Application**). You can name it whatever you like; we suggest naming it Space Pizza.

We will now create new Swift files in our Xcode project. Within Xcode, in the upper-left corner, you should be able to navigate to **File | New | File...**, which will bring up a window with a list of options (which you will see shortly).

Here is how you can navigate within Xcode to create a new Swift file:

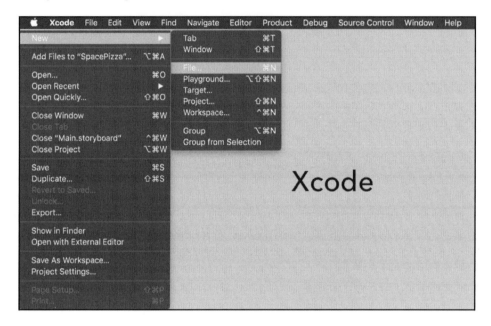

After finally selecting **File...** by going through the menu that we just listed, or by holding down the *command* key and pressing *N* (which does the same thing), you will be met with the following window:

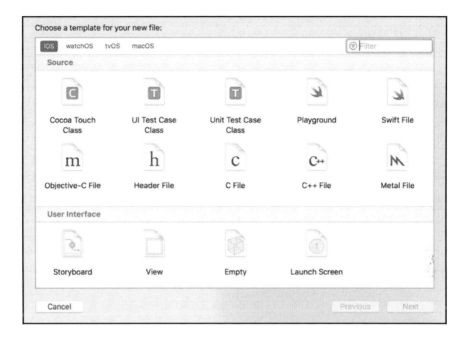

You will want to select **Swift File** before selecting **Next**. Make sure that **iOS** is selected at the top of this window, where it states **Choose a template for your new file:**. After selecting **Next**, you will be able to name your file. With this information, create three Swift files in your Xcode project, named:

- `Planet.swift`
- `PizzaService.swift`
- `SpaceJunk.swift`

After creating these three new files, select the `Planet.swift` file in the Project Navigator.

Before we write any code, let's talk a little about **enumerations**.

Enumerations

An enumeration defines a common type for a group of related values. What exactly does that mean? An enumeration defines a type (just like classes do) that we can use in our code. We can create an enumeration in Swift using the enum keyword followed by a pair of braces, as follows:

```
enum Direction {

}
```

All related source code for this chapter can be found here: https://github.com/swift-book-projects/swift-3-programming-for-kids/tree/master/Chapter-13.

This is identical to how we define new classes.

As of now, we've only defined a type by creating an enum, called Direction. We still have to create the group of related values. In this scenario, the group of related values that relate to Direction will be up, down, left, and right. We want to associate these four values with some sort of type (the type here being an enum called Direction). Here is how we associate those four values with Direction:

```
enum Direction {
    case up
    case down
    case left
    case right
}
```

You create various values that would be associated with an enum by writing out the keyword case followed by the value you want.

This enum—Direction, now has four different values associated with it.

If you want to create an instance of `Direction` in your code, you do so by first typing out the name of the type, followed by a period, and you can select one of the values from the ones provided, as shown:

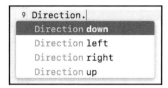

You first type out the name of the type. In this example, the name of our `enum` type is `Direction`. Following the type name, you should type out a period. After doing so, you will be met with the options you see in the preceding screenshot. Those options are `down`, `left`, `right`, and `up`.

Here is a screenshot of us creating two instances of `Direction` within a playground file:

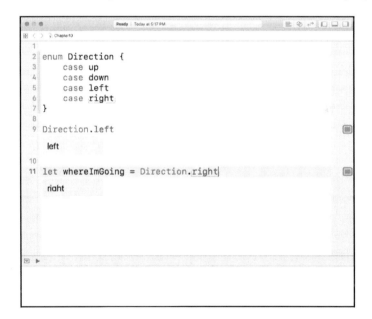

In the preceding screenshot, we've created a constant, `whereImGoing`, and assigned it the `Direction.right` value. Here, `whereImGoing` is of the `Direction` type and its value is `.right`.

Well, what can we do with this new constant now? A lot of times, when writing your code, you will come across situations just like this where you need a type in your code to represent a group of similar values (just like `Direction`). If we're creating a game, we might be interested to know which direction our user is moving in. If the user is moving `up`, then we will let them through the door, if the user is moving `right`, then they will face the villain! If they are moving `down`, then we will let them through the secret passage. There's an action we want to take depending upon the direction our user is moving in.

In Swift, we can write code to check our `whereImGoing` variable and see what value it has. We can do this by writing a chain of if-else statements, as illustrated:

```
let whereImGoing = Direction.right

if whereImGoing == Direction.up {
    print("You are free to pass.")
} else if whereImGoing == Direction.right {
    print("Sorry! It's time to fight your arch nemesis.")
} else if whereImGoing == Direction.down {
    print("Welcome to the secret room.")
}

// Prints "Sorry! It's time to fight your arch nemesis."
```

As you can see, what prints to console is `Sorry! It's time to fight your arch nemesis`. Why? This is because, when you step through the various if statements, you will find that we enter the set of braces following the `whereImGoing == Direction.right` because that statement evaluates to `true`.

Instead of solving this problem with an if-else statement, we can use what's referred to as a **switch** statement. Solving this problem like we just did using an if-else statement isn't wrong, in fact, it's doing exactly what we want it to do. However, it just doesn't look right; it looks kind of messy. This problem is better suited to a switch statement.

Switch statement

We can solve the same problem using a switch statement. The following code solves the exact same problem of seeing what direction our user is moving in, but by using a switch statement:

```
switch whereImGoing {
case .up:
    print("You are free to pass.")
case .right:
    print("Sorry! It's time to fight your arch nemesis.")
case .down:
    print("Welcome to the secret room.")
case .left:
    print("The unknown")
}

// Prints "Sorry! It's time to fight your arch nemesis."
```

You might note that we are handling the .left case as well. We didn't handle the .left case in our if-else statement in our earlier example (although we could have if we wanted to). When using a switch statement, it must be exhaustive. We have no choice in the matter. If you decide to switch on a variable, you have to account for every single possibility. There are only four possibilities when switching on whereImGoing: up, right, down, and left. In our example here, we are accounting for every case.

The switch statement works just like the if statement. We are inspecting the value of a variable and, depending on what the value is, we run some code. One difference here is that, within our switch statement, we don't need to include the Direction type. It's inferred that the type is Direction and it would be redundant to write out Direction (over and over), so you can omit the word and just write out case .up, case .right, as we did in the preceding code snippet.

When describing the value of an enum type, you can omit the type's name and just write out the specific case. For example, we would write .up, .down, .left, or .right if it is known that we're referring to the Direction type (ensuring that we include the period before the name of the case).

You might also note that there's another difference in comparing the `switch` statement to the if statement. The `switch` statement doesn't include any braces. You write out the `case` keyword followed by one of the cases of the `enum` type and it is followed by a colon. Any code written after that colon up to the next case will be executed if the case matches up with what's being switched on.

The value of `whereImGoing` is `.right`. When entering our `switch` statement, this matches up with the `case` `.right:` line of code, which means any code following this colon up to the next case statement (which is `.down` in our example) will be executed. This is how `Sorry! It's time to fight your arch nemesis.` prints to the console.

Planet

Next, we will implement another `enum`—`Planet` , which will represent all the various planets that our user will be able to select. Here is the code that we will be writing in our `Planet.swift` file:

```
enum Planet: String {

    static let all: [Planet] = [.mercury, .venus, .earth, .mars,
        .jupiter, .saturn, .uranus, .neptune]

    case mercury
    case venus
    case earth
    case mars
    case jupiter
    case saturn
    case uranus
    case neptune

    var lightMinutesFromEarth: Double {
        switch self {
        case .mercury: return 5
        case .venus: return 2
        case .earth: return 0
        case .mars: return 4.5
        case .jupiter: return 35
        case .saturn: return 71
        case .uranus: return 152
        case .neptune: return 242
```

```
        }
    }

    var displayName: String {
        return rawValue.capitalized
    }

}
```

 Enumerations in Swift can have functions. They can also have computed properties (which is what `lightMinutesFromEarth` and `displayName` are in the preceding code).

We will step through this code line by line. If you haven't already done so, navigate to the `Planet.swift` file that we created earlier. You will want to start out by defining the `Planet` type and providing it with the following cases:

```
enum Planet: String {

    case mercury
    case venus
    case earth
    case mars
    case jupiter
    case saturn
    case uranus
    case neptune

}
```

What's really cool (which we didn't talk about earlier) is that you could have also created this `enum` type not by having to write case over and over, as follows:

```
enum Planet: String {

    case mercury, venus, earth, mars, jupiter, saturn, uranus, neptune

}
```

But wait! What's this : `String` we added at the end of `Planet`? What does that do?

It's what's referred to as a **raw value**. Raw values can be strings, characters, or any of the integer or floating-point number types. Here, the raw value for the Planet, enum is defined to be of the String type.

Our cases in our Planet enum type now have all raw values associated with their case name. This means that Planet.mercury has a raw value of mercury, Planet.venus has a raw value of venus, and so on.

What does it mean to have a raw value?

The rawValue property is available to all instances of the Planet type (because we provided it with a raw value of String at declaration). Note that we didn't create this property ourselves; it just exists by virtue of being an enum. Each instance of Planet has its own rawValue property that contains a value. The value being the String version (letter for letter match) of the case. Here is an example of us creating an instance of Planet and accessing that instance's rawValue instance property:

```
let myFavPlanet = Planet.earth
print("I love (myFavPlanet.rawValue)")
// Prints "I love earth"
```

Here, myFavPlanet is a constant of the Planet type with a value of .earth. Following this constant is a print statement that uses string interpolation. We're accessing the rawValue property available to the myFavPlanet instance, which in turn will return the String value earth.

If rawValue returns a String value, then there's nothing stopping us from using any methods available to String on it. Here is an example of calling a method available to String instances on the rawValue instance property, which is itself a String:

```
let myFavPlanet = Planet.earth
print("I love (myFavPlanet.rawValue.uppercased()) and I want to
tell the world!")
// Prints "I love EARTH and I want to tell the world!"
```

Here, we're calling the uppercased() method on our String value (which is what rawValue gives us), which will end up being EARTH in this example.

Next, we should create a computed property, `displayName`, of the `String` type, which should return `rawValue.capitalized`. Here is that code:

```
var displayName: String {
    return rawValue.capitalized
}
```

To see this in action, let's create a new instance of `Planet` and print out the `displayName` property available to it:

```
let bigPlanet = Planet.jupiter
print("(bigPlanet.displayName) is a large planet.")
// Prints "Jupiter is a large planet.
```

Now, every instance of `Planet` has a `displayName` computed property available to it. As you can see, in this example, where we're using `.jupiter`, `displayName` returns the value `Jupiter`.

Next, we will create another computed property, called `lightMinutesFromEarth`, of the `Double` type. Here is that code:

```
var lightMinutesFromEarth: Double {
    switch self {
    case .mercury: return 5
    case .venus: return 2
    case .earth: return 0
    case .mars: return 4.5
    case .jupiter: return 35
    case .saturn: return 71
    case .uranus: return 152
    case .neptune: return 242
    }
}
```

This computed property is making use of a `switch` statement. It begins by switching on `self`. What exactly is happening here?

Well, we know that when you `switch` on a variable, you check to see which case matches up with the value of the variable. You can think of `self` here as being a variable whose value is equal to the value of the instance that called on this computed property. They are one and the same.

Here, we are creating a new instance of `Planet` and assigning it to a constant named `thirdRockFromTheSun`:

```
let thirdRockFromTheSun = Planet.earth
```

Here, `thirdRockFromTheSun` is a constant of the `Planet` type with a value of `.earth`. If `thirdRockFromTheSun` (being an instance of `Planet`) was to call on its `lightMinutesFromEarth` computed property (which it has available to it because, again, it's an instance of `Planet`), then `self` would be equal to `.earth`.

Here, we will store the value returned to us by `lightMinutesFromEarth` into a constant called `minutes`:

```
let minutes = thirdRockFromTheSun.lightMinutesFromEarth
print("We are (minutes) light minutes away.")
// Prints "We are 0.0 light minutes away."
```

Also, if you were to step through that `switch` statement in this example, we match up with the `.earth` case within the `switch` statement because `self` is equal to `.earth`. This is how we get back the `0.0` value, which is evident in our preceding print statement.

Type property

We have one more piece of code to write before we move on. The following is a constant, `all`, declared with the `static` keyword:

```
static let all: [Planet] = [.mercury, .venus, .earth, .mars, .jupiter,
.saturn, .uranus, .neptune]
```

We've created a static constant, named `all`, of the `[Planet]` type.

A type property (created using the `static` keyword) is a property available only to the type itself. Let's pretend that we have a toy factory that creates instances of toys. Well, imagine that the toy factory had properties of its own. As in, a factory might have its own address. It might be a big building with its own color. These properties available to the factory are considered type properties and we create them in Swift using the `static` keyword. The properties associated with the factory (as in its address and color) are separate/different from the properties available to the toys that this factory creates.

Let's go back to our static property called `all`. How do we access this type property that is only available to the `Planet` type itself and not instances of `Planet` (like `.mercury` or `.mars`.)? Here is how we do that in code:

```
Planet.all
```

That's it; it's that easy. You type out the name of the type, followed by a period, and you should see listed any and all properties available to the type (in this case, there is only one). Also, you should see all cases you can select to create an instance of `Planet`. However, we don't want to do that, we want to select `all`. By doing this, we're getting back the array of `Planet`, which is stored in this constant named `all`.

Let's store this value in another constant that we will call `allThePlanets` to see how this is working. We will also loop through this array of `Planet` and print out each value to the console to see that this is indeed working as we expect:

```
let allThePlanets = Planet.all

for planet in allThePlanets {
    print(planet.displayName)
}

/* Prints
 Mercury
 Venus
 Earth
 Mars
 Jupiter
 Saturn
 Uranus
 Neptune
*/
```

We will be writing no more code in our `Planet.swift` file. This `enum` is complete!

Space junk

Navigate to the `SpaceJunk.swift` file. Before we begin writing any code, let's have a little chat about space debris.

According to NASA, there are more than 20,000 pieces of debris larger than a softball orbiting the Earth. They travel at speeds of up to 17,500 mph (28,000 kmph), fast enough for a relatively small piece of orbital debris to damage a satellite or a spacecraft. There are 500,000 pieces of debris the size of a marble or larger. There are many millions of pieces of debris that are so small that they can't be tracked.

Considering that we deliver pizza from Earth to all the other planets in our solar system, we have to be safe about how we get there. Considering that our delivery spacecraft can move at the speed of light, there are certain precautions that need to be taken if there is a highly unusual amount of space debris out there.

The Earth's government keeps track of the levels of space debris out there in our solar system. There are three different levels: low, medium, and high.

Before looking at the answer (which you will find ahead), try to complete the following instructions to give yourself a challenge:

1. Create an enum named `SpaceJunk` with a raw value of the `String` type.
2. The three cases that should be created in this enum are `low`, `medium`, and `high`.
3. Define a computed property named `displayName` of the `String` type. In your implementation of this computed property, you should try to return a `String` value that represents the name of the case, but is capitalized.

After making an attempt to create this `enum` from the preceding instructions, you should try to compare how you did with the following answer:

```
enum SpaceJunk: String {

    case low, medium, high

    var displayName: String {
        return rawValue.capitalized
    }

}
```

We now have a `SpaceJunk` enum, which we will be using shortly. Now, let's talk about our `PizzaService` class.

Pizza service

Navigate to the `PizzaService.swift` file. We will go through each line of code here, implementing our own custom `PizzaService` type.

This class will be the main class that controls our application. It will act as a real-life pizza service, where it will have a name and will be able to produce the costs associated with delivering pizza to certain planets. The following code is the completed implementation of the `PizzaService` type (note that the `didSet` observer which you will see implemented in the following code snippet is something we will be covering in the coming pages):

```
class PizzaService {

    let name: String

    private var pricePerLightMinute = 20.0

    var spaceJunk: SpaceJunk = .low {
        didSet {
            switch spaceJunk {
            case .low: pricePerLightMinute = 10.0
            case .medium: pricePerLightMinute = 20.0
            case .high: pricePerLightMinute = 50.0
            }
        }
    }
}
```

```
    init(name: String) {
        self.name = name
    }

    func deliveryCharge(for destination: Planet) -> Double {
        return pricePerLightMinute *
destination.lightMinutesFromEarth
    }

}
```

First, you should begin by defining a new class type (within the `PizzaService.swift` file) named `PizzaService`, as follows:

```
class PizzaService {

}
```

Next, you should create a constant, `name`, of the `String` type. Right below this constant, you should create an `init` function that takes in one argument, labeled `name`, of the `String` type. In your implementation of the `init` function, you should assign the `name` parameter to `self.name`.

We have to use `self` within the `init` function. This is because we need to distinguish between our property called `name` and the arguments label, which is also called `name`. The compiler wouldn't even let us write `name = name` if we wanted to. We need to distinguish between the two by writing `self.` before the name of the instance's property we're referring to.

This is what your code should look like right now:

```
class PizzaService {

    let name: String

    init(name: String) {
        self.name = name
    }

}
```

Next, you should create a variable, `pricePerLightMinute`, which will be of the `Double` type. Considering that we're assigning a default value to this property, we can take advantage of type inference. You don't need to supply this variable with any type information, but assign it with a default value of `20.0`. As we've assigned this variable with a default value (one that represents a `Double` type, by virtue of us including the decimal in the number), we don't need to supply it with any explicit type information. This is known as type inference.

One more thing–include the keyword `private` before the `var` keyword in your creation of this variable, as shown:

```
private var pricePerLightMinute = 20.0
```

Your `PizzaService` class should now look like this:

```
class PizzaService {

    let name: String

    private var pricePerLightMinute = 20.0

    init(name: String) {
        self.name = name
    }

}
```

What does that `private` keyword do? The `private` keyword is used when we want to disallow any instance of the type (that would normally be created in another file) from accessing that particular instance property.

You can also mark your functions with the `private` keyword.

To show you how this works, we will navigate to the `ViewController.swift` file (note that you don't have to follow along for this example) and create an instance of `PizzaService` in the `viewDidLoad()` method. We will store this `PizzaService` instance in a constant called `testService`. It's `name` property will be `Jessica's Pizza Palace`:

```
override func viewDidLoad() {
    super.viewDidLoad()
    let testService = PizzaService(name: "Jessica's Pizza Palace")
}
```

If we were to make an attempt to use this `testService` instance by typing a period after it, we would be met with the following output:

```
let testService = PizzaService(name: "Jessica's Pizza Palace")
testService.
   V  String name
```

Note that, when we type out the word `testService` followed by a period, Xcode is able to show us everything available for us to use. We can only access the instance's `name` property and not `pricePerLightMinute`. That's because we marked the `pricePerLightMinute` property with the `private` keyword. Only `name` is available for us to use here.

Why would we do this? For starters, it makes writing code safer. What if we want to create an instance property that doesn't need to be accessible to any instance but will be used internally within the definition of the class? What if we want to ensure that no one (outside of the class that it belongs to, in our implementation of the type) can change this property? We ensure these things by marking the variable with the `private` keyword. By doing so, note how, when we were looking at the properties and methods available to us through `testService`, we were only able to see the `name` instance property in the preceding screenshot.

Note that you didn't need to be following along with us in Xcode for this example. If you were following along, you should remove any code that you've written within the `viewDidLoad()` function in the `ViewController.swift` file.

At this point, you should navigate back to the `PizzaService.swift` file.

Next, you should implement a function, `deliveryCharge(for:)`, which takes in one argument, labeled as `destination`, of the `Planet` type. This function should return a `Double` value. In your implementation of this function, you should try to provide a solution to the following problem. We want to know how much we should charge our customers when we receive orders that require us to deliver pizza across the galaxy to a specific planet.

Considering that we have a price we charge per light minute (`20.0`), let's provide a solution to the problem. This method has one argument, labeled `destination`, of the `Planet` type. We know that a `Planet` instance has a `lightMinutesFromEarth` property. This property is of the `Double` type. Our `pricePerLightMinute` property is also of the `Double` type. In order to figure out the price we need to charge a customer, we need to multiply these two values. We should return the result of the `pricePerLightMinute *` `destination.lightMinutesFromEarth` statement.

Here's what our `PizzaService` class currently looks like:

```
class PizzaService {

    let name: String

    private var pricePerLightMinute = 20.0

    init(name: String) {
        self.name = name
    }

    func deliveryCharge(for destination: Planet) -> Double {
        return pricePerLightMinute *
destination.lightMinutesFromEarth
    }

}
```

The next thing we should do is implement a new property, called `spaceJunk`.

We know that there are three levels associated with how much space junk is out there in the solar system. Those three levels are `.low`, `.medium`, and `.high`. Depending on the level, our price per light minute should go up. Why? It's because it's more dangerous! The following list is a breakdown of the space junk level and the corresponding price per light minute:

- Low: $10.00
- Medium: $20.00
- High: $50.00

So, when the `spaceJunk` level changes, our `pricePerLightMinute` should also change, but how can we tie the two together? If `spaceJunk` is set to `.high`, then the `pricePerLightMinute` property should be `50.0`. It should match up with the schedule we just provided. How do we provide a solution to this problem in code? One way is to use **property observers**.

Property observers

A property observer is a block of code (think of a block of code as the code that executes in between braces `{ }`) that executes when the value of a specific instance property changes. You create property observers within your declaration of an instance property. When that instance property's value changes, the property observer created within it executes.

Lets go right into the code and step through it line by line to make sure that we understand what a property observer is. The following code snippet is our current implementation of `PizzaService`, which now includes the property observer within our `spaceJunk` instance property. Note how `spaceJunk` also has a default value of `.low`:

```
class PizzaService {

    let name: String

    private var pricePerLightMinute = 20.0

    var spaceJunk: SpaceJunk = .low {
        didSet {
            print("Hello Universe!")
            }
    }

    init(name: String) {
        self.name = name
    }

    func deliveryCharge(for destination: Planet) -> Double {
        return pricePerLightMinute * destination.lightMinutesFromEarth
    }

}
```

Can you see how we create property observers now? It looks more confusing than it really is. If you have a firm grasp of what problem property observers are solving, then that is a great start! Don't feel that you should understand how to use them fully by seeing them here for the first time. It takes practice, and then it takes more practice! Don't be ashamed to have to revisit topics over and over when learning how to code.

Right after the `.low` default value, you can see that we created a new set of braces. Within the scope of those braces, we can create property observers:

- `willSet` is a property observer that is called just before the value is stored
- `didSet` is a property observer that is called immediately after the new value has been stored

You create a property observer by typing either the `willSet` or `didSet` keyword, followed by a set of braces. Within the scope of those braces, all the code you write will only execute when the value of the instance property it's written within changes.

Let's go through a quick example (you don't need to write this code anywhere). Here, we have a constant, `mikesPizza`, of the `PizzaService` type. Its value is a `PizzaService` instance with the `Mike's Pizza` name. Here is that code:

```
let mikesPizza = PizzaService(name: "Mike's Pizza")
```

Let's now change the `spaceJunk` property on `mikesPizza` to a different value, twice! Here, we are changing the `spaceJunk` instance property to `.medium` and then to `.high`, as shown:

```
mikesPizza.spaceJunk = .medium
mikesPizza.spaceJunk = .high
```

We've first changed the `spaceJunk` value to `.medium`. Then, on the following line of code, we changed the `spaceJunk` value to equal `.high`. Changing this value twice would have had the `didSet` property observer we created earlier execute twice. This means that "`Hello Universe!`" would have printed to the console twice.

This is a really powerful tool!

Now, knowing this, we don't want to just print `Hello Universe!` to the console, we want to update our `pricePerLightMinute` property to equal a different value depending on what the `spaceJunk` property was changed to (which could either be `.low`, `.medium`, or `.high`). This sounds like a problem that could be solved using a switch statement! Things are starting to come together.

The following is our fully implemented `PizzaService` type. We've added a `switch` statement inside our `didSet` observer. Here is that code:

```
class PizzaService {

    let name: String

    private var pricePerLightMinute = 20.0

    var spaceJunk: SpaceJunk = .low {
        didSet {
            switch spaceJunk {
            case .low: pricePerLightMinute = 10.0
            case .medium: pricePerLightMinute = 20.0
            case .high: pricePerLightMinute = 50.0
            }
        }
    }

    init(name: String) {
```

```
        self.name = name
    }

    func deliveryCharge(for destination: Planet) -> Double {
        return pricePerLightMinute * destination.lightMinutesFromEarth
    }

}
```

Now, anytime the value of our `spaceJunk` property is changed, the `didSet` observer we just created is called (or executed). In its execution, we enter a `switch` statement that begins by switching on `spaceJunk` itself (which is the property that we're in!). We know that this `didSet` observer is executed after the value of the `spaceJunk` property has been changed. This means, when we `switch` on `spaceJunk`, whatever its value is represented as what it was just changed to. So, if it was just changed to `.low`, then we will enter the `.low` case (as they match) and the code within that case will be executed. Sticking to this example, `switch` will execute the following piece of code:

```
    pricePerLightMinute = 10.0
```

That's incredible! It's changing the value of our private variable, `pricePerLightMinute`. Even though it's marked as `private`, we can still access it within the `PizzaService.swift` file. It's protected in that we can only use it within this file and nowhere else. This makes it very safe–no one can accidentally assign a value to this property without us knowing about it.

Now, anytime someone changes the value of our `spaceJunk` property, the `pricePerLightMinute` will have its value changed, as it will reflect the price it should be at the space junk level that satisfies our preceding question.

Storyboard and view controller

Navigate to the `Main.storyboard` file. This is where we will design our iOS application.

From the object library, you should drag out a `UIPickerView` and place it near the bottom of the screen. After doing that, you should drag out three `UIButton` objects and place them above the `UIPickerView`. We've changed the opacity of the three buttons, along with their titles. At the top of the screen should be a `UILabel` with its text set to **Delivery Cost**. Below this `UILabel` should be another `UILabel` with its text set to **$0.00**. We've changed the background colors of the buttons and labels. You can design it however you like!

The following is a screenshot of how we designed the application:

Feel free to skip the part of setting up all the constraints on the various view items (for now). Note, though, that this is something you shouldn't ignore if you want to finalize this application (meaning, release it to the App Store). We will provide a brief summary as to how we went about setting up our constraints, but know that this isn't typically how you would solve this problem. Meaning, someone won't be giving you a list of instructions to follow to set up your various views. While you're learning constraints, there is a lot of trial and error in becoming comfortable with them. Based upon how the views are laid out, you should be able to get some sense as to the constraints that need to be added. Be warned though, this isn't an easy task. Generally, you add one view at a time and constrain that one view before adding another to the hierarchy. Feel free to try to add your own constraints without making reference to the following cheat sheets.

Cheat sheet for `UIPickerView`:

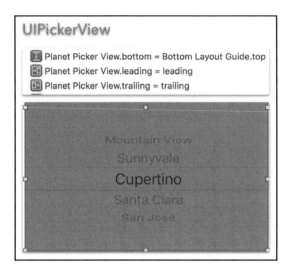

Cheat sheet for `UILabels`:

Cheat sheet for `UIButtons`:

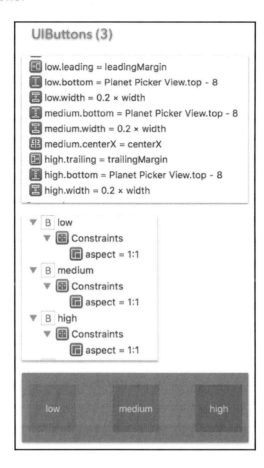

Hooking everything up

In the Identity Inspector in the upper-right hand corner, set the **Class** to `ViewController`. This now connects our view controller scene (which contains all our buttons and labels) with our `ViewController.swift` file. The following screenshot gives us a closer look:

Next, you will want to bring up the Assistant Editor because we will want to create a connection between these UIView objects we've created in our View Controller Scene with the `ViewController.swift` file. This will allow us to update what is being displayed to our user in code.

To bring up the Assistant Editor, hold down *command + option* and then hit the *return* key. To hide the Assistant Editor, while holding down the *command* key, press the *return* key. That is how you can hide and un-hide the Assistant Editor.

Now, you will want to control drag from your `UIPickerView` you have in the View Controller Scene to the `ViewController.swift` file (preferably at the top). After doing so, you will be asked to name it. You should name this outlet `planetPickerView`.

Next, you should create an outlet from the `UILabel` which will represent the total cost we will want to display to the user. While holding down control, drag from the `UILabel` down to the `ViewController.swift` file and name this outlet `costLabel`.

After completing those two tasks, your `ViewController.swift` file should contain the following two `IBOutlets`:

```
@IBOutlet weak var planetPickerView: UIPickerView!
@IBOutlet weak var costLabel: UILabel!
```

This allows us, within the scope of our `ViewController` class, to access any of these variables that connect to the view objects users will see on screen when the app launches.

Below these variables, you should create two new instance properties, as shown:

```
var selectedPlanet = Planet.mercury
let franksPizza = PizzaService(name: "Franks Pizza")
```

We're making use of the custom types we made earlier. Here, `selectedPlanet` is a variable where we're assigning it a default value of `Planet.mercury`. This means that `selectedPlanet` is of the `Planet` type, with its value being `.mercury`. As it's declared as a variable, we can change its value to whatever we want later on. This variable will keep track of what planet the user has currently selected on screen. When a user changes the planet (by scrolling through the various planets in our `UIPickerView`), this variable will change to reflect that. We will write this code shortly.

The `franksPizza` constant is of the type `PizzaService`. We're assigning it a default value, being an instance of `PizzaService` with its name set to `Franks Pizza`. We will be utilizing `franksPizza` throughout the various methods in our `ViewController` class. We will be calling on the `deliveryCharge(for:)` method on our `franksPizza` instance when a user changes the space junk level and/or the selected planet. That method call returns to us a `Double` value representing the cost. We will be displaying this cost to the user in our `costLabel`. We will be stepping through this in detail shortly.

Navigate to the top of your `ViewController.swift` file. Once you see the declaration of the `ViewController` class, you should add `UIPickerViewDataSource` and `UIPickerViewDelegate` to the right of where you see `UIViewController`. It should wind up looking like this:

```
class ViewController: UIViewController, UIPickerViewDataSource, UIPickerViewDelegate {
```

So, what exactly did we do here? `UIPickerViewDataSource` and `UIPickerViewDelegate` are two protocols. You can think of protocols as promises. And by writing protocols after your declaration of a type, as we did, we are stating that we are making a promise.

If we made a promise to our mom that we would take out the trash, we would better take out the trash, no matter what! Our making the promise to our mom that we will do something is us adopting a protocol. Us actually taking the trash out is conforming to the protocol.

So, when we write out `UIPickerViewDataSource` and `UIPickerViewDelegate`, as we just did, we are adopting two separate protocols. We are making the promise that we will do something. These promises are slightly more complicated than taking out the trash though.

When you make a promise in code, you need to implement a certain function or create a specific variable. You can think of this as taking out the trash or satisfying the promise you made.

Let's start with `UIPickerViewDataSource`. When we make this promise, we need to implement the following two functions:

```
func numberOfComponents(in pickerView: UIPickerView) -> Int {

}

func pickerView(_ pickerView: UIPickerView, numberOfRowsInComponent
    component: Int) -> Int {

}
```

We first promised our mom that we will indeed take out the trash; now, this is us taking out the trash. However, you should note something. Both these functions return an `Int` value. We haven't implemented these functions yet, their bodies are empty.

Our `UIPickerView`, which we've decided to call `planetPickerView` when we created the `IBOutlet`, needs to know how many components and rows it needs to display to the user. This is how we tell it how many. We only want 1 component, which you can think of as a section. You can have different sections with different headers, but we're only displaying one group of items here (planets). The number of rows we want to display represents the number of items we want to display. In our case, we want to list all the planets, so the number of planets to display is what we should return in our second function, which is 8.

Your code should now look like this:

```
func numberOfComponents(in pickerView: UIPickerView) -> Int {
    return 1
}

func pickerView(_ pickerView: UIPickerView, numberOfRowsInComponent
    component: Int) -> Int {
    return Planet.all.count
}
```

Wait a minute! We're not returning the number 8 in that second function as we said we would. We're instead returning `Planet.all.count`. If you recall from earlier, we created a `static` property on the `Planet` type, called `all`, which looks like this:

```
static let all: [Planet] = [.mercury, .venus, .earth, .mars,
    .jupiter, .saturn, .uranus, .neptune]
```

After we get back the array value that contains all the planets, if we call on the `count` property (available to all the instances of array), we will get back the number of items that exist inside the array. In this case, there are 8 items in this array, so by returning `Planet.all.count`, it evaluates to 8, so we're really returning 8 here.

Now, add the following line of code to the `viewDidLoad()` method:

```
planetPickerView.dataSource = self
```

The `self` instance represents the current instance of `ViewController`. The `dataSource` property is of `planetPickerView` (which is an instance of `UIPickerView`). We are setting this property to equal the current instance of `ViewController`. It's connecting two instances to allow them to communicate to each other. Think of it as establishing a conversation that can now be had.

The following is a diagram that may make it easier to see how this conversation is had:

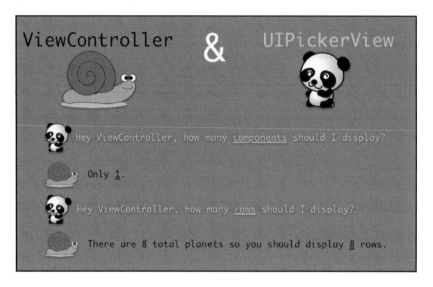

To enable and allow this conversation to take place, you need to write the preceding line of code in your `viewDidLoad()` method. The snail in our diagram represents `self` and the panda represents `planetPickerView`.

Next, we should talk about `UIPickerViewDelegate`. This is the second promise we've made.

 `UIViewController`, which is the first keyword we see after the declaration of our `ViewController` type, is not a protocol. The first item after a colon represents the **superclass** (which you can think of as being the parent).

The `UIPickerViewDelegate` promise is a little different. We will be required to implement the following functions:

```
func pickerView(_ pickerView: UIPickerView, titleForRow row:
  Int, forComponent component: Int) -> String? {

}

func pickerView(_ pickerView: UIPickerView, didSelectRow row:
  Int, inComponent component: Int) {

}
```

The first function we will implement has a return type of String?. This means that we can either return a String value, such as Blue or Red, or we can return the value nil, which is the equivalent of stating that we're returning nothing. We have a choice in the matter. Note that we won't be returning nil in our example.

Our implementation of these two functions will look like this:

```
func pickerView(_ pickerView: UIPickerView, titleForRow row:
   Int, forComponent component: Int) -> String? {
      let planet = Planet.all[row]
      return planet.displayName
}

func pickerView(_ pickerView: UIPickerView, didSelectRow row:
   Int, inComponent component: Int) {
      selectedPlanet = Planet.all[row]
}
```

Let's go through the first function listed, pickerView(_:titleForRow:forComponent:). This function will be called 8 times because this continues part of the conversation we created earlier in our diagram. The pickerView(_:numberOfRowsInComponent:) function, whatever it returns (we have it returning 8), is the same as the amount of times the pickerView(_:titleForRow:forComponent:) function can get called. Where the user is scrolling within the UIPickerView will decide what the value of the row argument will be.

 If you're ever confused as to how something is working or when something gets called, you should add print statements throughout your code to get a good sense of when a function gets called. Also, you should print out the various arguments to a function within the implementation of that function to see what their values are when your program runs.

Add the following line of code to the viewDidLoad() function in addition to what you had written earlier when setting the dataSource of the planetPickerView equal to self:

```
planetPickerView.delegate = self
```

This allows for the following conversation to take place:

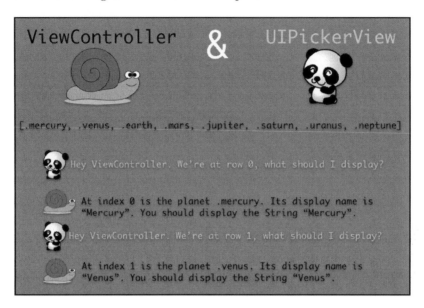

Our instance of `UIPickerView` and `planetPickerView` will call on
the `pickerView(_:titleForRow:forComponent:)` function 8 times. The preceding
diagram shows that the panda is asking the snail what to display, providing it with the
`row` value. The snail (or `ViewController`) can take this `row` value and look up the specific
value at that index in the array of planets that we can access through `Planet.all`. Using
subscript syntax (that is, `Planet.all[0]`), we can access certain values from this array by
index. That's how we use the `row` argument–we use it as an index accessing specific planets
from the `Planet.all` array. The specific planet accessed via index (or `row` in this case) is
stored in a constant called `planet`. Then, we return the `displayName` property on
the `planet` constant that represents the `String` value to be displayed to the user.

The second function should be implemented as follows:

```
func pickerView(_ pickerView: UIPickerView, didSelectRow row:
  Int, inComponent component: Int) {
    selectedPlanet = Planet.all[row]
}
```

This function is called whenever our user stops scrolling through the `UIPickerView` and picks a planet. Whenever a user decides to stop scrolling, this method will fire off. As soon as it does, the `row` argument of this function is all we're concerned with. Why? This is because where ever the user stopped scrolling, this `row` argument will reflect that. If the user stops scrolling and this function fires off where the `row` argument is equal to 0, then we know that the user stopped scrolling on Mercury. If the user scrolls all the way down to the bottom, this method will fire off and the `row` argument will be equal to 7. This means that the user has selected Neptune. We use this to our advantage. We update the `selectedPlanet` instance property to reflect this change. We have it equal to whatever `Planet.all[row]`, which will reflect exactly where the user stopped scrolling and the planet they have selected returns to us.

Space junk buttons

Navigate back to the `Main.storyboard` file. Now bring up the Assistant Editor again. We will want to create an `IBActions`, making a connection between our `UIButton` and our `ViewController.swift` file.

Drag the button from the left-most `UIButton` (which we labeled as `low`) and create an `IBAction` in the `ViewController.swift` file, calling the function `lowSpaceJunkChange`. Then, create a separate `IBAction` from the middle `UIButton` and call the function `mediumSpaceJunkChange`. Lastly, create an `IBAction` from the third `UIButton` and call the function `highSpaceJunkChange`. After doing this, it should look as follows:

```
@IBAction func lowSpaceJunkChange(_ sender: Any) {
}

@IBAction func mediumSpaceJunkChange(_ sender: Any) {
}

@IBAction func highSpaceJunkChange(_ sender: Any) {
}
```

Now we need to implement these three functions. Depending on which `UIButton` the user taps on, the `IBAction` tied to that specific `UIButton` will fire off. When a user taps on one of the `UIButton`, depending on which `UIButton` was tapped, we will update the `spaceJunk` instance property on `franksPizza`. For example, if someone taps on the low button, then we should update the `frankPizzas` class' `spaceJunk` property to equal `.low`. If we were then to follow through with that change, we would also see that there's a `didSet` observer written within the scope of the `spaceJunk` instance property in the `PizzaService.swift` file that will fire off.

Considering we just updated this property to equal `.low`, we will fall within the `.low` case, where we will then change the `pricePerLightMinute` instance property to `20.0`. All of this takes place as soon as a user taps on one of the three `UIButton`, how awesome! Here's a screenshot of us implementing the `mediumSpaceJunkChange(_:)` function, where we're ensuring that the `spaceJunk` property will be set to `.medium`:

```
59    @IBAction func lowSpaceJunkChange(_ sender: Any) {
60        franksPizza.spaceJunk = .low
61    }
62
63    @IBAction func mediumSpaceJunkChange(_ sender: Any) {
64        franksPizza.spaceJunk = .
65    }                        SpaceJunk high
66                            SpaceJunk low
67    @IBAction func h                            er: Any) {
68    }                        SpaceJunk medium
69
```

As you can see, in updating the `spaceJunk` property, we have three options to change it to (being that `SpaceJunk` is an `enum` type with three cases). Here, we're updating it to the `.medium` value, in that we're writing this code within the `mediumSpaceJunkChange(_:)` function and a user would have just tapped the medium space level button.

After you're done updating each `IBAction` with the appropriate code, it should look like this:

```
@IBAction func lowSpaceJunkChange(_ sender: Any) {
    franksPizza.spaceJunk = .low
}

@IBAction func mediumSpaceJunkChange(_ sender: Any) {
    franksPizza.spaceJunk = .medium
}

@IBAction func highSpaceJunkChange(_ sender: Any) {
    franksPizza.spaceJunk = .high
}
```

The next thing we need to do is update the cost and show the user what the new cost is. When a user either taps on one of the three buttons or changes the selected planet to a different planet, we should update the cost label to reflect what that new price is.

Updating the cost

Let's solve the problem of updating the label with the new price by creating a new function. This new function will be called `updateCost()` and it will not take in any arguments or return any values. It will look like this:

```
func updateCost() {
    let cost = franksPizza.deliveryCharge(for: selectedPlanet)
    let numberFormatter = NumberFormatter()
    numberFormatter.numberStyle = .currency
    let number = NSNumber(floatLiteral: cost)
    let costText = numberFormatter.string(from: number)
    costLabel.text = costText
}
```

The first thing we need to do in our implementation of this function is create a new constant, named `cost`, and assign it the return value of a call to `franksPizza.deliveryCharge(for: selectedPlanet)`. The `selectedPlanet` value at that time (which would be whichever planet is selected within the `UIPickerView`) will be what is passed into this function call. If we go through our implementation of the `deliveryCharge(for:)` function implemented within the `PizzaService.swift` file, we will see that the following line of code will run:

```
return pricePerLightMinute * destination.lightMinutesFromEarth
```

This function call will return `pricePerLightMinute`, which is a private variable of the `Double` type. It's of the `Double` type because we assign it a default value of `20.0` and, through type inference, Swift is able to figure out that the number literal `20.0` can be inferred to be of the `Double` type. We take this value and multiply it by `destination.lightMinutesFromEarth`. `destination` is the name of our argument and we are accessing an instance property on it, called `lightMinutesFromEarth`. Depending on what our `destination` is, which is of the `Planet` type, we are looking to see how far away it is from Earth because that goes into the cost of how much we want to charge our customer. We take this value and multiply it by `pricePerLightMinute`, which is determined by how much space junk there is in the solar system. If the `spaceJunk` property on a `PizzaService` instance is set to `.low`, `pricePerLightMinute` is equal to `10.0`, if it's set to `.medium`, the value is `20.0`, and if it's set to `.high`, it's equal to `50.0`. The result of this multiplication is what is returned to the caller of this function.

On our next line of code, we are creating a new constant called `numberFormatter` and assigning it a value being an instance of the `NumberFormatter` type. An instance of this type can convert textual representations of numeric values. We have a `Double` value that we would like to convert to a `String`. Not only that, we would like our `Double` value to display in the currency format. If our `cost` constant is equal to 20.0 (for example), then we would like to display this to the user as $20.00. An instance of `NumberFormatter` can do this conversion for us.

Next, we need to do a little setting up of our `numberFormatter` constant. We should update its `numberStyle` stored property to equal `.currency`. This will allow for the 20.0 value to be turned into $20.00. After updating this property, we should create a new constant called `number` and assign it a value being an instance of `NSNumber`. The `NSNumber` type has many init functions available for us to use. We are looking for the one that takes in a `Double` as its argument (as that is the type of our `cost` constant, above which we will be passing to it). Calling on `NSNumber(floatLiteral:)`, you should pass in the `cost` constant as its argument. In doing so, an instance of `NSNumber` will be created and stored in the `number` constant. The reason we are doing this is that, in order to convert a numeric value into a `String`, the argument to the function that will be doing this work for us asks that, the type of the argument be of type `NSNumber` (which you will see shortly).

Lastly, create a constant called `costText` and assign it a value being equal to the return value we receive from a call to the `string(from:)` method available to instances of `NSNumberFormatter`. In calling on this function, we will pass it the `number` constant (as the argument of this function is of type `NSNumber`). After doing this, our `costText` constant is of type `String` and should represent the delivery charge (in currency format) we will be charging our customer. With this information, we can now update our `costLabel` by updating its `text` property to equal `costText`. In doing this, this will update the `UILabel` displayed on screen.

Now we need to use the `updateCost` function we just made.

All our `IBAction` should now call `updateCost` after they update the `spaceJunk` property on `franksPizza`. This should now look like this:

```
@IBAction func lowSpaceJunkChange(_ sender: Any) {
    franksPizza.spaceJunk = .low
    updateCost()
}

@IBAction func mediumSpaceJunkChange(_ sender: Any) {
    franksPizza.spaceJunk = .medium
    updateCost()
```

```
    }

    @IBAction func highSpaceJunkChange(_ sender: Any) {
        franksPizza.spaceJunk = .high
        updateCost()
    }
```

Now, anytime one of the three `UIButton` are tapped on, we will update the `spaceJunk` property accordingly, and then call our `updateCost()` function, which will change the cost label to reflect the new price.

There's only one more line of code we need to write. There's another place that a user can do something in our app where we will need to change the price and update the cost label–it's when they select a different planet. We are currently updating the cost when a user taps on one of the three `UIButton`, but we're not accounting for when they might change the `selectedPlanet` to a different planet.

If you recall from earlier, this change (or update) occurs when the following method fires off (note that the following method now includes the `updateCost()` call), which is something you should add:

```
func pickerView(_ pickerView: UIPickerView, didSelectRow row:
  Int, inComponent component: Int) {
    selectedPlanet = Planet.all[row]
    updateCost()
}
```

When `pickerView(_:didSelectRow:inComponent:)` fires off, due to the fact that the user has just scrolled through the `UIPickerView` and changed it to a different planet, we will want to update the cost label. We call on our `updateCost()` method here as well, because the price will now be different.

This is the finished product after we've selected **Jupiter** (with **medium** space junk) when running the app:

Summary

Congratulations on completing this project! This is no small feat; you've just created your first iOS application. We've introduced a lot of new topics, which include the following:

- Enumerations
- Enumerations with raw values
- Private variables
- didSet observers
- Adopting and conforming to a Protocol
- UIPickerView
- Switch statements
- The amount of light minutes from Earth to all the other planets

If there ever comes a time when you will be delivering pizza in space, you will have a head start with this app. Maybe not; we first have to figure out a way to travel at the speed of light. Maybe you can figure that out!

The next and final chapter will have you creating another application to store your favorite movies. This application will work on generating a list and displaying it in a `UITableViewController`.

14
Movie Night - iOS App

Congratulations on making it to the final chapter! In this chapter, we will look at one more useful pattern when creating iPhone apps–making lists using the `UITableViewController` type. Lists are very popular in apps since they are an intuitive way of illustrating a list of items. These items can then be added, deleted, or perhaps you can select them to reveal more information about a specific item.

After looking at how you can create a list for your app, we will use that knowledge to build one last app–the Movie Night application. This application will use some of the knowledge we have gained throughout the book, while taking advantage of the pattern of creating lists. Toward the end of the chapter, we will quickly look at how we can install our application on our iPhone so that we are able to carry the application with us, making it easier to show it to our friends and family.

To sum up, this chapter will cover the following topics:

- An introduction to how one can create lists in iPhone applications using the `UITableViewController` type
- Guiding the reader on how to create the Movie Night application to handle one's favorite movies
- How to install the application on an iPhone device

How to create a list

Creating lists is very common in the real world, as well as in software applications. A list in a software application can be used for a variety of things, such as creating a to-do list, showing a list of the most recent news, or showing the items on the menu of your local pizza joint:

A list in an iOS application is most commonly implemented, and referred to, as a table view. A table view refers to the `UITableView` UI element, which is the view that gives us a list of horizontal items. Each item in the list is referred to as a **cell** due to its type being `UITableViewCell`. A cell comes with a set of predefined formats, but custom cells can also be created to fit the developer's needs. Further, a list can be divided into sections, for example, by the first letter of a contact's last name, as in the preinstalled **Contacts** app that ships with iOS:

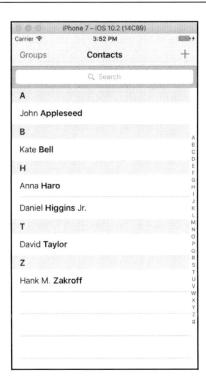

Besides setting up the interface to include the `UITableView`, a set of methods needs to be implemented in the corresponding `UIViewController`. These methods will ensure that data is able to be displayed and will tell the application how it should handle user interaction with the table view. In fact, there are two protocols that are very relevant to conform to in order to set up a list. A protocol defines a set of variables and/or a set of functions a conforming object needs to implement in order to satisfy the protocol. In relation to setting up a list, conforming to two protocols is necessary to make it work correctly. These two protocols are named `UITableViewDataSource` and `UITableViewDelegate`.

The data source

The data source, or the `UITableViewDataSource` protocol to be more precise, has some required methods that you need to implement in order to conform to the protocol. The protocol also defines a set of optional methods that one can implement for more control of the table view. Let's go through some of the most popular methods.

The first method has the following signature:

```
func numberOfSections(in tableView: UITableView) -> Int
```

This method should return a value of the `Int` type, which should indicate how many sections there are in the table view. If we take a look at the screenshot from Apple's **Contacts** app, we can see that this table view has five sections. This method will return 1 by default if you do not implement it.

The next method says something about how many rows exist in each section. The signature looks as follows:

```
func tableView(_ tableView: UITableView, numberOfRowsInSection section:
Int) -> Int
```

As the method name indicates, this method will state how many rows should go into each section in the `UITableView`. For example, in the preceding screenshot from the **Contacts** app, there should be one row for the first section. The first section is **A** and the single row is **John Appleseed**.

Another central method from the `UITableViewDataSource` protocol has the following signature:

```
func tableView(_ tableView: UITableView, cellForRowAt indexPath: IndexPath)
-> UITableViewCell
```

This method looks a little different than the others because it does not say anything about the number of sections, rows, or similar that is needed in order to set up the table. Instead, it prepares the actual view for the cell that has the `UITableViewCell` type, as explained earlier. This means that the view this method returns will be the actual cell for that specific row. Looking at the screenshot of the **Contacts** app, we can see that each cell is fairly simple and only contains one label that shows the name of the contact.

The delegate

While the `UITableViewDataSource` protocol tries to encapsulate the required data in order to display the table view, the `UITableViewDelegate` protocol tries to encapsulate what should happen when a user interacts with the table view. The `UITableViewDelegate` protocol does not have any required methods, but a long list of optional methods. Let's take a look at one of the most used methods. It has the following signature:

```
func tableView(_ tableView: UITableView, didSelectRowAt indexPath:
IndexPath)
```

As the name of the method indicates, this method will be called when a user taps on a row in the list. The developer will then be able to react based on that; for example, by displaying more information about the specific item.

UITableViewController

Up until now, we have looked at how we can make our `UIViewController` show a list using the `UITableView` by conforming to the two protocols: `UITableViewDataSource` and `UITableViewDelegate`. However, there's a slightly different approach one can take to make a list, that is, to make a `UITableViewController` instead of a `UIViewController`. The difference is that the `UITableViewController` inherits from `UIViewController`, which means that it acts like a view controller, but it also gives you some list-related functionality out-of-the-box.

First of all, it comes with the `UITableView` already placed in the interface. It also implements all the required related methods with some default behavior. This means that all we need to do in order for it to work as we want, is to implement the relevant methods. Let's take a look at how to do this by developing one last application: Movie Night.

Our final application: Movie Night

The final application we will make is called **Movie Night** and the idea of the app is to be able to write down one's favorite movies:

The interface will have a couple of different elements. First of all, the view will have a title in the top middle. In the upper-right corner, there will be a small button with a plus symbol on it, which will enable the user of the app to add a movie to the list. The main area of the application will contain a list of the added movies. When the user swipes from right to left on a specific item in the list, a button with the **Delete** label will appear; tapping that button will make the item on the list disappear.

In general, unless one has a strategy for saving data either on the phone or through a web interface, the data will be lost when the user closes the app. This means that all the movies one might have added to the list will disappear the second the user closes the app. To avoid this, we will write some simple code that will *persist* the added movies. This will enable us to save any added movies before closing the app, as well as to load these movies again when the app is opened.

The interface

Create a new (**Single View Application**) project in Xcode and name it **Movie Night**. Save the project in a place on your hard drive where you will be able to locate it again. Remember that the description of how to create a project can be found in `Chapter 11`, *Simon Says*.

Then, open `Main.storyboard` and select **View Controller** on the canvas:

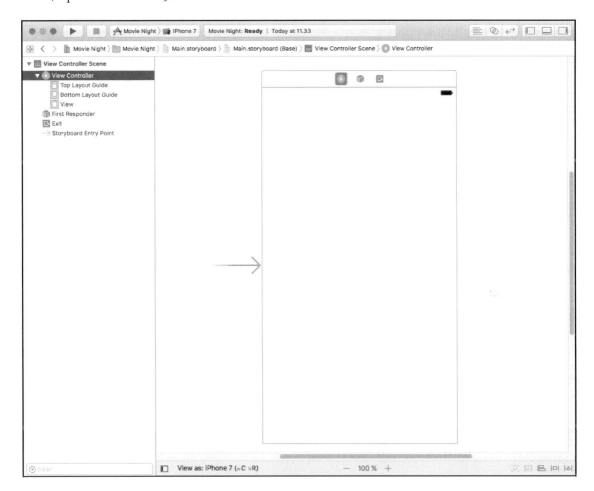

 All related source code for this chapter can be found here: `https://github.c om/swift-book-projects/swift-3-programming-for-kids/tree/master/C hapter-14`.

Having selected that, we will press *Backspace* on the keyboard in order to delete it from the canvas. After deleting that, we will try and find the **Table View Controller** from the **Object Library** at the lower right-hand side of Xcode (in the Utilities area):

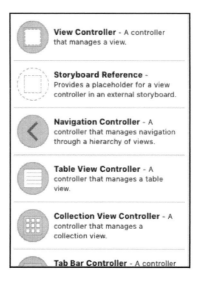

Next, we will drag a table view controller into the canvas. Then, to ensure that this view will be the first we see when we run our application, we will select our newly added table view controller and ensure that **Is initial View Controller** is checked in the **Attributes Inspector**:

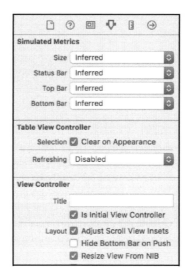

Running our application at this point should give us an application with an empty list we can scroll by swiping up and down:

At this point, Xcode will give us a minor warning relating to a missing identifier on our cell in our list. To fix this, we click on our cell, which is the area with the **Prototype Cells** label in our canvas. Then, in the **Attributes Inspector**, there's a field with no value that has the **Identifier** label. This will be an identifier for the particular cell we are creating. The identifier may become useful when we want to add dynamic values to our cells in code. In this text field, go ahead and type in MovieCell as our identifier.

At the same time, change the **Style** of our cell from **Custom** to **Basic**. This is a built-in style for our cell that will give us one label (similar to the cell displayed in the **Contacts** app):

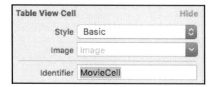

In order to add a title and the plus button to our application, we need to add something called a navigation controller. To do this, we will select our table view controller and then, in the menu bar, navigate to **Editor** | **Embed In** | **Navigation Controller**:

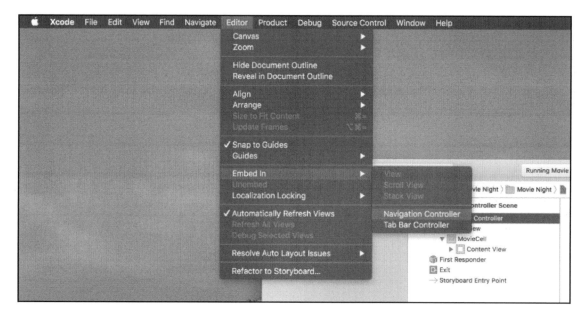

This should add a navigation controller to the canvas, making our canvas look like this:

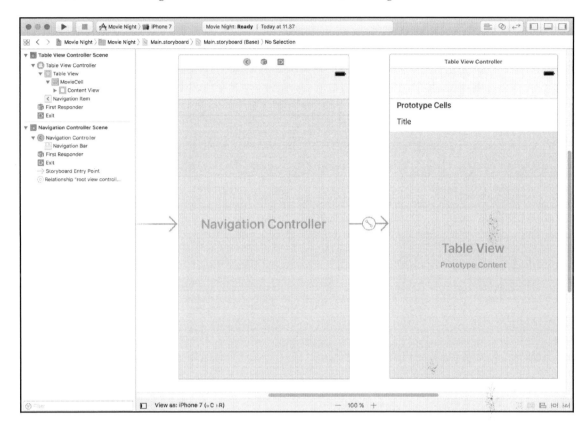

If we now run our application, we can see that a navigation bar (the gray area above the list) has been added to our application:

We are already making great progress with our UI. Let's add the final touches before moving on to our code.

Next, we will specify a title for our application by double-clicking on the gray area in the navigation bar in our table view controller. This will reveal a small input field where we can type in `Movie Night`. To the right of the title, we will drag a **Button** from the **Object Library** that will be the button to add a movie. After placing the button, the style of the button can be changed to **Done** and the **System Item** can be changed to **Add** in order to get the built-in plus symbol button. This should give you a canvas like this:

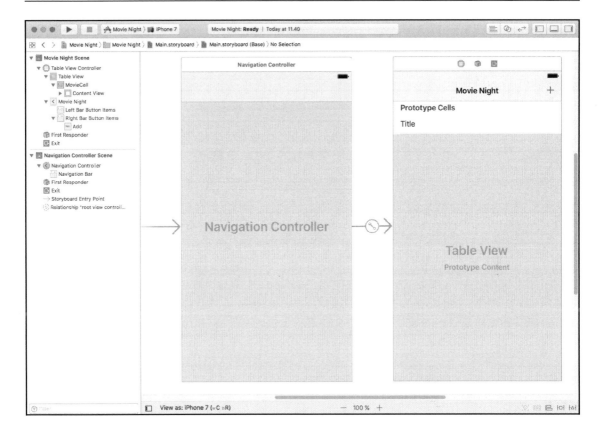

One last thing to do before we start coding is to add a function for our button. Before we can do this, we need to ensure that there is a proper link between our `ViewController.swift` and our new table view controller on our canvas. First, open up `ViewController.swift` and remove the following line:

```
class ViewController: UIViewController {
```

In its place, insert the following line:

```
class ViewController: UITableViewController {
```

This will indicate that our view controller is now a `UITableViewController`. Open up `Main.storyboard` again and select our table view controller. Then, in the Utilities area, we will take a look in the **Identity Inspector**. Here, we type in `ViewController` as the **Class** for our table view controller:

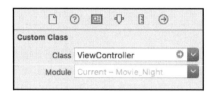

With that in place, we can now click on the **Show the Assistant editor** button (with the two circles) in the upper-right corner to let Xcode display the canvas and a code editor side by side. Then, as we did in Chapter 12, *Starry Night*, we will hold *Ctrl* while left-clicking on the button (with the plus symbol), dragging the cursor into our source editor, and then we will release the left-click right before the last } in our code. We will then change the connection to an Action and name it `addTapped`. This should us leave with the following content in our `ViewController.swift`:

```
import UIKit

class ViewController: UITableViewController {

    override func viewDidLoad() {
        super.viewDidLoad()
        // Do any additional setup after loading the view, typically from a
nib.
    }

    override func didReceiveMemoryWarning() {
        super.didReceiveMemoryWarning()
        // Dispose of any resources that can be recreated.
    }


    @IBAction func addTapped(_ sender: Any) {
    }
}
```

With this in place, we can now look at how we can display items in our list.

Displaying items in our list

With the interface in place, we are now ready to add the code for our application. Before getting started, go ahead and remove the `didReceiveMemoryWarning()` method from our `ViewController.swift`, as we will not be using this method.

Then, the first thing we will do is to introduce a variable that will hold our movies:

```
var movies: [String] = []
```

Our movies will be an array of strings that will correspond to the titles of the movies and, initially, our list will be empty, until a user adds a movie to the list.

Next, we will add the required methods defined in the `UITableViewDataSource` and `UITableViewDelegate` protocols to display data in our list:

```
override func tableView(_ tableView: UITableView, numberOfRowsInSection
section: Int) -> Int {
    return movies.count
}

override func tableView(_ tableView: UITableView, cellForRowAt indexPath:
IndexPath) -> UITableViewCell {
    let cell = tableView.dequeueReusableCell(withIdentifier: "MovieCell",
for: indexPath)
    cell.textLabel?.text = movies[indexPath.row]
    return cell
}

override func tableView(_ tableView: UITableView, didSelectRowAt indexPath:
IndexPath) {
    tableView.deselectRow(at: indexPath, animated: true)
}
```

Note how we have added the `override` keyword. This is required because we are now inheriting from `UITableViewController`, which already has these methods defined.

The first method simply returns the amount of movies we have in our variable. The number of cells in the list will then correspond to the number of movies in our variable.

The second method will try to create a cell using the identifier we specified in our canvas and then set the title of the label to the title of the movie we have stored in our `movies` array.

When creating a `UITableView`, we can enhance the performance of our application by limiting the number of views created for our list by reusing cells. This makes a lot of sense since we are often unable to show all items in our list onscreen at the same time. The method `dequeueReusableCell(withIdentifier:)` tries to find a cell that can be reused; if not found, it will create a new one.

The last method will simply deselect any selected row in the list, as we will not be adding any functionality for when the user taps on a row in the list.

By separating our code using `// MARK:`, it can become a bit easier to grasp our code. At this point, your `ViewController.swift` should look like this:

```swift
import UIKit

class ViewController: UITableViewController {

    var movies: [String] = []


    // MARK: View life cycle

    override func viewDidLoad() {
        super.viewDidLoad()
        // Do any additional setup after loading the view, typically from a
nib.
    }


    // MARK: UITableViewDataSource

    override func tableView(_ tableView: UITableView, numberOfRowsInSection
section: Int) -> Int {
        return movies.count
    }

    override func tableView(_ tableView: UITableView, cellForRowAt
indexPath: IndexPath) -> UITableViewCell {
        let cell = tableView.dequeueReusableCell(withIdentifier:
"MovieCell", for: indexPath)
        cell.textLabel?.text = movies[indexPath.row]
        return cell
    }


    // MARK: UITableViewDelegate
```

```
        override func tableView(_ tableView: UITableView, didSelectRowAt
    indexPath: IndexPath) {
            tableView.deselectRow(at: indexPath, animated: true)
        }


        // MARK: IB Actions

        @IBAction func addTapped(_ sender: Any) {

        }
    }
```

We are now very close to being able to display something in our list; all we need is values in
our movies array.

Dynamically adding items to our list

If our movies array contained any items, we would have everything in place to display
items in our list. However, let's move on and look at how we can add items to our list using
our button with the plus symbol. To do this, we will use something called a
UIAlertController, which will help us display a small popup, in this case, to add a
movie. Following our movies declaration, go ahead and add the given line:

```
let alert = UIAlertController(title: "Add movie", message: "What movie do
you want to add?", preferredStyle:.alert)
```

Now that we have an instance of an UIAlertController, we can present that to the user
when tapping on the add button. To present the alert, add the following code inside our
already-created addTapped(_ sender: Any) method:

```
present(alert, animated: true, completion:nil)
```

Now, when we run our application, we should be able to see our popup when we click on
the button with the plus symbol; however, there is no way to add a title for our movie, nor
any way of dismissing the popup. To fix this, we will introduce a small helper function to
add the required functionality to our alert:

```
func setupAddMovieAlert() {
    // Setup textfield
    alert.addTextField()

    // Action for add
    alert.addAction(UIAlertAction(title: "Add", style: .default) { action
 in
```

```
            guard let text = self.alert.textFields?.first?.text else {
                return
            }
            guard text.characters.count > 0 else {
                return
            }

            // Reset textfield
            self.alert.textFields?.first?.text = ""

            // Add movie
            self.movies.append(text)
            self.tableView.reloadData()
        })

        // Action for cancel
        alert.addAction(UIAlertAction(title: "Cancel", style: .cancel, handler:
    nil))
    }
```

This helper can be broken into three steps:

1. Add a text field to type in the title of a movie.
2. Add the functionality that should be fired when we want to add a movie. In this
   case, we're checking, using a guard statement, to see that some text has been
   entered to avoid adding movies with no titles. A guard statement is useful for
   making sure a value with an optional type has a value, but can also be used for
   comparisons. Basically, it says "if this is not true then do this", which in this case
   will return from our function. After that, we ensure that we delete whatever has
   been entered in the field so that it appears empty the next time the user wants to
   add another movie. Lastly, we ensure that we add the movie to our array of
   movies and reload our table view so that our newly added movie appears in the
   list.
3. Add the functionality that should be fired when we want to cancel adding a
   movie. Since the default behavior for the action is to close the popup, there's no
   need to add any extra code in this case.

In order for this code to be run, we should remember to call the helper function inside our `viewDidLoad()` method. Our code should now look like this:

```swift
import UIKit

class ViewController: UITableViewController {

    var movies: [String] = []
    let alert = UIAlertController(title: "Add movie", message: "What movie do you want to add?", preferredStyle:.alert)


    // MARK: View life cycle

    override func viewDidLoad() {
        super.viewDidLoad()

        setupAddMovieAlert()
    }


    // MARK: UITableViewDataSource

    override func tableView(_ tableView: UITableView, numberOfRowsInSection section: Int) -> Int {
        return movies.count
    }

    override func tableView(_ tableView: UITableView, cellForRowAt indexPath: IndexPath) -> UITableViewCell {
        let cell = tableView.dequeueReusableCell(withIdentifier: "MovieCell", for: indexPath)
        cell.textLabel?.text = movies[indexPath.row]
        return cell
    }


    // MARK: UITableViewDelegate

    override func tableView(_ tableView: UITableView, didSelectRowAt indexPath: IndexPath) {
        tableView.deselectRow(at: indexPath, animated: true)
    }


    // MARK: IB Actions

    @IBAction func addTapped(_ sender: Any) {
```

```
            present(alert, animated: true, completion:nil)
    }


    // MARK: Helpers

    func setupAddMovieAlert() {
        // Setup textfield
        alert.addTextField()

        // Action for add
        alert.addAction(UIAlertAction(title: "Add", style: .default) {
action in
            guard let text = self.alert.textFields?.first?.text else {
                return
            }
            guard text.characters.count > 0 else {
                return
            }

            // Reset textfield
            self.alert.textFields?.first?.text = ""

            // Add movie
            self.movies.append(text)
            self.tableView.reloadData()
        })

        // Action for cancel
        alert.addAction(UIAlertAction(title: "Cancel", style: .cancel,
handler: nil))
    }
}
```

If we run our application and click on the button with the plus symbol, we should see the following screen:

After entering a title for a movie and clicking on **Add**, it should appear in the list:

As soon as you add more items to the list than can be displayed, you will be able to scroll by swiping up and down.

Deleting items from our list

Adding functionality for deleting movies in our list can be a fairly easy task, since a lot of it is built-in. In fact, all we have to do is to add a method from the `UITableViewDelegate` protocol, like this:

```
override func tableView(_ tableView: UITableView, commit editingStyle:
UITableViewCellEditingStyle, forRowAt indexPath: IndexPath) {
    guard editingStyle == .delete else {
        return
    }
    movies.remove(at: indexPath.row)
    tableView.deleteRows(at: [indexPath], with: .fade)
}
```

This will then enable the swiping gesture that will make it possible for a user to swipe from right to left and then press the **Delete** button in order to delete a movie from the list. The two lines toward the bottom ensure that the selected movie is deleted from our array of movies and removed from the table view using a fade animation.

If you add a movie and then try to swipe from right to left on that specific movie, the **Delete** button should be slowly revealed:

After pressing the **Delete** button, the movie should disappear from the list.

Persisting our movies

As you might have already noted, if you add movies, close the app and then reopen it, the movies are gone. This is because the movies are stored in memory and, as soon as we close the app, all the data related to the app will be deleted. To overcome this, we will persist the movies in a small database so that when we reopen the app, the movies will still be there. For this, we will introduce two helper methods: one for saving movies and one for loading movies.

First, we need to add a small constant to the top of our `ViewController.swift`, right where we declared our `movies` array and our `alert` constant:

```
let storageKey = "myMovies"
```

This will be our identifier for saving and loading our movies. Then, we will add the following method for saving movies:

```
@objc func saveMovies() {
    UserDefaults.standard.setValue(movies, forKey: storageKey)
    UserDefaults.standard.synchronize()
}
```

This method simply uses a small database, which can be accessed by calling `UserDefaults.standard`. We use this database to store a value (being our movies) using the key we have just defined (`storageKey`). Then, to complete our store operation, we need to remember to call `synchronize()`.

Next, we will add a method to load movies:

```
func loadMovies() {
    guard let movies = UserDefaults.standard.array(forKey: storageKey) as?
[String] else {
        return
    }
    self.movies = movies
}
```

This method tries to load our array of movies from the same database using our key, and if it is not to be found, we just return from the function. If we find our movies in the database, we will assign them to our `movies` variable so that we can use that to set up our table view.

The last thing we need to do is consider when to call these two methods. Loading movies makes sense as soon as our view loads (in `viewDidLoad()`); however, when to save our movies can be a bit tricky. As `viewWillDisappear(_:)` (as explained in Chapter 12, *Starry Night*) won't be called in any scenarios where our view gets out of focus, we need to find another approach. Basically, what we want is to save our movies every time our application becomes inactive, either because it was put into the background, or because it was closed completely. To do this, we can add the following code to `viewDidLoad()`:

```
NotificationCenter.default.removeObserver(self, name:
  .UIApplicationWillResignActive, object: nil)
NotificationCenter.default.addObserver(self, selector:
#selector(saveMovies),
  name: .UIApplicationWillResignActive, object: nil)
```

The first line ensures that we are not already observing for notifications based on when the app becomes inactive. The next line will ensure that we get notifications when the application becomes inactive. When the application becomes inactive, we want our `saveMovies()` method to be called, which is specified using the `#selector()`, which also explains why we needed to add the `@objc` keyword to our `saveMovies()` function. The reasons for this are not important at this point.

Your complete code in `ViewController.swift` should now look like this:

```swift
import UIKit

class ViewController: UITableViewController {

    var movies: [String] = []
    let alert = UIAlertController(title: "Add movie", message: "What movie
do you want to add?", preferredStyle:.alert)
    let storageKey = "myMovies"


    // MARK: View life cycle

    override func viewDidLoad() {
        super.viewDidLoad()

        // Setup app notifications
        NotificationCenter.default.removeObserver(self, name:
.UIApplicationWillResignActive, object: nil)
        NotificationCenter.default.addObserver(self, selector:
#selector(saveMovies), name: .UIApplicationWillResignActive, object: nil)

        // Setup add movie alert
        setupAddMovieAlert()

        // Load movies
        loadMovies()
    }


    // MARK: UITableViewDataSource

    override func tableView(_ tableView: UITableView, numberOfRowsInSection
section: Int) -> Int {
        return movies.count
    }

    override func tableView(_ tableView: UITableView, cellForRowAt
indexPath: IndexPath) -> UITableViewCell {
```

```
        let cell = tableView.dequeueReusableCell(withIdentifier:
    "MovieCell", for: indexPath)
        cell.textLabel?.text = movies[indexPath.row]
        return cell
    }


    // MARK: UITableViewDelegate

    override func tableView(_ tableView: UITableView, didSelectRowAt
    indexPath: IndexPath) {
        tableView.deselectRow(at: indexPath, animated: true)
    }

    override func tableView(_ tableView: UITableView, commit editingStyle:
    UITableViewCellEditingStyle, forRowAt indexPath: IndexPath) {
        guard editingStyle == .delete else {
            return
        }
        movies.remove(at: indexPath.row)
        tableView.deleteRows(at: [indexPath], with: .fade)
    }


    // MARK: IB Actions

    @IBAction func addTapped(_ sender: Any) {
        present(alert, animated: true, completion:nil)
    }


    // MARK: Helpers

    func setupAddMovieAlert() {
        // Setup textfield
        alert.addTextField()

        // Action for add
        alert.addAction(UIAlertAction(title: "Add", style: .default) {
    action in
            guard let text = self.alert.textFields?.first?.text else {
                return
            }
            guard text.characters.count > 0 else {
                return
            }

            // Reset textfield
```

```
            self.alert.textFields?.first?.text = ""

            // Add movie
            self.movies.append(text)
            self.tableView.reloadData()
        })

        // Action for cancel
        alert.addAction(UIAlertAction(title: "Cancel", style: .cancel,
handler: nil))
    }

    func loadMovies() {
        guard let movies = UserDefaults.standard.array(forKey: storageKey)
as? [String] else {
            return
        }
        self.movies = movies
    }

    @objc func saveMovies() {
        UserDefaults.standard.setValue(movies, forKey: storageKey)
        UserDefaults.standard.synchronize()
    }
}
```

If you run the application now, add some movies, close it, and then reopen it, you should be able to still see all our movies. You now have an application to keep track of your favorite movies; good job!

Deploying our application to our iPhone

Before ending this chapter, let's quickly go through how to run our Movie Night application on a real iPhone. To do this, we need to ensure that we have the following things in place:

- The iPhone is connected to the computer using a Lighting to USB cable
- You have an Apple ID account

Then, by navigating to **Xcode | Preferences** and then selecting the **Accounts** tab, you should be able to click on **+** in the lower-left corner of the window. There, you will have an option to **Add Apple ID...**.

After entering your Apple ID details, you can close the preferences window and click on **Movie Night** in the **Navigator** area on the left:

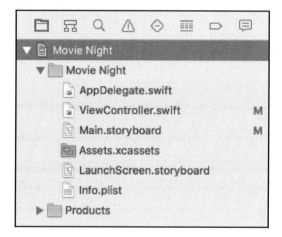

This will bring up the general settings for your project. The second section will be named **Signing**; in this section, you should be able to choose your Apple ID as the **Team**:

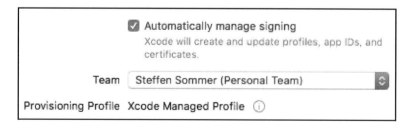

After selecting this, you should be able to select your iPhone as the device and hit play to install it on your phone. If Xcode mentions something about verification of the developer app certificate, then just follow the onscreen steps and try to install the application again.

Summary

Wow, you just created an application to store your favorite movies! The application persists your movies and you are able to install the application on your phone so that you are able to bring it with you and show it to your friends and family. Good job!

This chapter introduced lists using the `UITableView` and `UITableViewController` types. We looked at the two related protocols—`UITableViewDataSource` and `UITableViewDelegate`—and some of the most central methods defined in these protocols. We then looked at how to set up an interface that uses a table view and how we can populate lists using the `UITableViewController`. We added a navigation controller in order to set a title for our app and to have a place for adding a button to add items to our list. We also looked at how we can delete items from the list using swipe gestures. Lastly, we looked at how we can persist data using `UserDefaults` so that our items stay in the list even after we close our app. We combined all this into our Movie Night app, which we then installed on a physical iPhone, as opposed to the iPhone simulators in Xcode.

Throughout this book, a lot of central concepts to iOS programming have been covered. We hope that it has been a fun and educative journey into the world of programming and we hope that you are interested in continuing this journey. Trust us when we say that, although we have covered a lot, there is still a lot to learn, which makes programming so exciting.

Index